Kawaii Crochet Dolls

AMIGURUMI PATTERNS FOR 10 ADORABLE DOLLS AND 30 CUTE CHARACTERS

Elise Brocard

DAVID & CHARLES
— PUBLISHING —

www.davidandcharles.com

My name is Elise. I live in a small village in the Haut-Doubs region of France with my husband and our two kids, Noah and Éléonore.

I have always been fascinated by the manga universe, which has been a great source of inspiration to me. Ever since I was young, I have loved designing things to make. I went on to study fashion design, where I was able to bring my clothing designs to life.

I discovered crochet during my first pregnancy. I started by following patterns made by other creators, but I soon took the plunge and created my first doll, Aya. Since then, I have gotten a huge amount of pleasure from imagining, designing, and crocheting dolls and their outfits.

Today my dream has come true! I could never have imagined that one day I would have my own book. I am so happy to share this wonderful adventure with you. For my first book, I wanted to revisit my earliest creations. I have loved this opportunity to revisit my early days as a creator. I hope you enjoy meeting Aya, Kitsune, and all the others. I have put my heart into this book, and I hope you will have a great time in the company of all these cute dolls.

Happy crocheting!

Elise

Instagram: @ptitepeste.amigurumi
Website: ptitepeste.com
Etsy: ptitepeste.etsy.com

Contents

Materials

Hooks

All the dolls are crocheted using a size US 4 (2.00mm) hook. Some details are worked using a size US 4/0 (1.75mm) or a US F-5 (3.75mm) crochet hook.
It is important to adapt the size of your hook and the thickness of your yarn to your individual crocheting style. This will ensure that the stuffing will not show through the stitches. Personally, I use the ergonomic crochet hooks made by Tulip, which are very pleasant to handle and of excellent quality.

Yarn

All the projects in this book have been crocheted using yarn from the brand Yarn and Colors:

- Must-Have (100% mercerized cotton, 1¾oz (50g), 137yds (125m))
- Furry (100% polyester, 1¾oz (50g), 82yds (75m))
- Glamour (100% polyester, ¾oz (20g), 172yds (158m))

I like these yarns both for their quality and for their attractive color palette. All the colors, types of yarn, and quantities are given for each doll, but you can choose to use any yarn and colors you like.

Stuffing

I used synthetic fiberfill in all these projects.
It is important to stuff firmly and evenly. I use the flat side of a metal crochet hook to help slip in small amounts of fiberfill at a time.

Basic Tool Kit

You will need the following for all the projects in this book:

- embroidery floss: white, black, brown, blue, and/or purple
- chenille stems
- aluminum wire, diameter 0.06in (1.5mm)
- aluminum wire, diameter 0.02in (0.5mm)
- small pliers (optional)
- stitch markers
- yarn needle
- pair of scissors
- pins
- blush

For Aya, Tenshi, and Mimi you will also need a toothpick.

Safety Eyes

I use 7mm plastic safety eyes from the Etsy shop, SnacksiesHandicraft.
If the doll is intended for a child under the age of three years, I recommend embroidering the eyes.

Glue

For sticking cotton to cotton, I use the all-purpose glue made by Prym. It is a solvent-free textile glue that becomes transparent when it dries. You can, of course, use any sort of textile glue.
For sticking cotton to a toothpick or aluminum wire, I use Super Glue made by Loctite. It is a transparent glue that sticks numerous materials instantly.

2/0
LOCTITE
SUPER GLUE

Basic Stitches

Crochet Basics

SLIP KNOT (THE STARTING KNOT)

1. With the hook behind the yarn, form a loop following the arrow.
2. Trap the loop you have made with your thumb, then wrap the yarn round the hook.
3. Draw the yarn through the loop you made in Step 1.
4. Pull the end of the yarn downwards in order to tighten the loop.

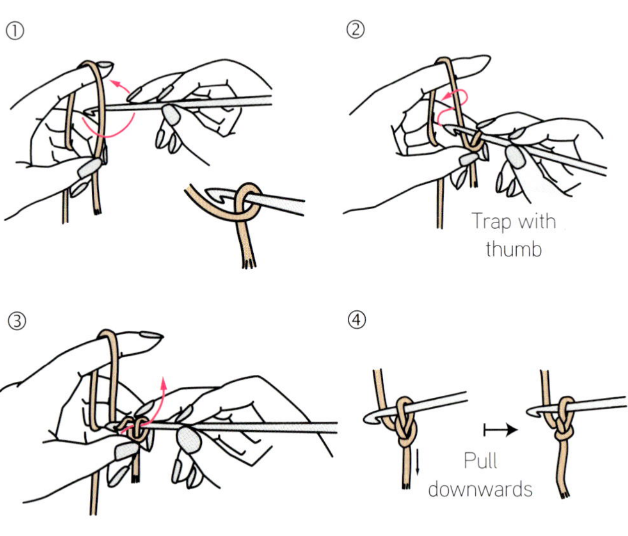

MAGIC RING

1. Wrap the yarn around your index finger twice, then insert the hook through the loops and draw the yarn back through.
2. Yarn round hook, then draw the loop on to the hook. Your magic ring is complete

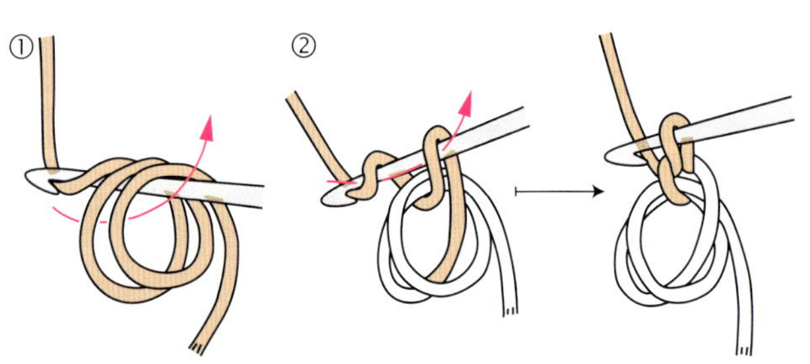

CHAIN STITCH

1. Wrap the yarn round the hook from back to front.
2. Draw the yarn through the loop of the starting knot, making the first chain stitch.
3. Yarn round hook and draw through the loop to form the second chain stitch.
4. Continue working in this way until you have the required number of stitches.

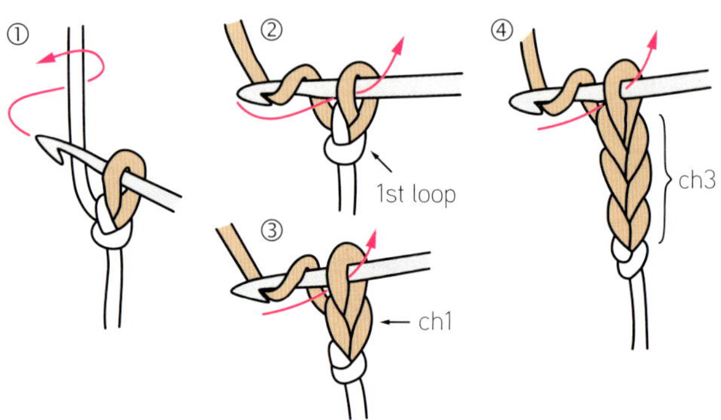

SLIP STITCH

1. Insert the hook into the first stitch from front to back.
2. Yarn round hook, then draw through the stitch.
3. Insert the hook into the second stitch from front to back.
4. Continue working in this way for the required number of stitches.

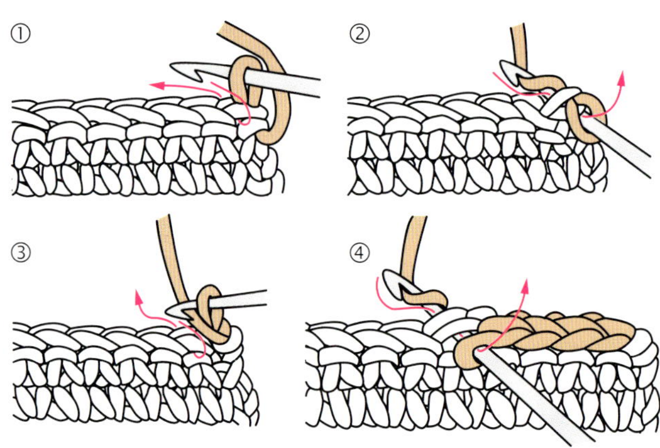

SINGLE CROCHET

1. Insert the hook into the back of the chain as shown by the arrow.
2. Yarn round hook, then draw through the loop, as shown by the arrow.
3. Yarn round hook again, then draw through both loops on the hook, as shown by the arrow.
4. Continue working in this way, repeating Steps 1–3 as many times as required. On following rows, work into the two strands at the top of each stitch instead of the back of the foundation chain (unless working X-shaped single crochet stitches).

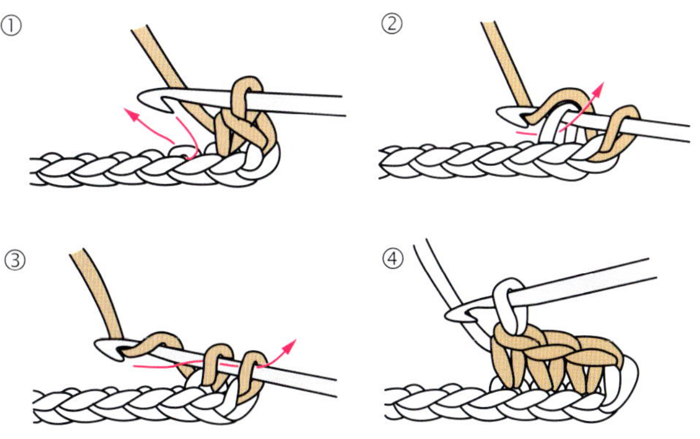

DOUBLE CROCHET

1. Yarn round hook, then insert the hook into the back of the chain as shown by the arrow.
2. Yarn round hook, then draw through the loop, as shown by the arrow.
3. Yarn round hook, then draw through two loops on the hook as shown by the arrow.
4. Yarn round hook, then draw through the two remaining loops on the hook.

Repeat Steps 1–4 as many times as required. On following rows, work into the two strands at the top of each stitch instead of the back of the foundation chain.

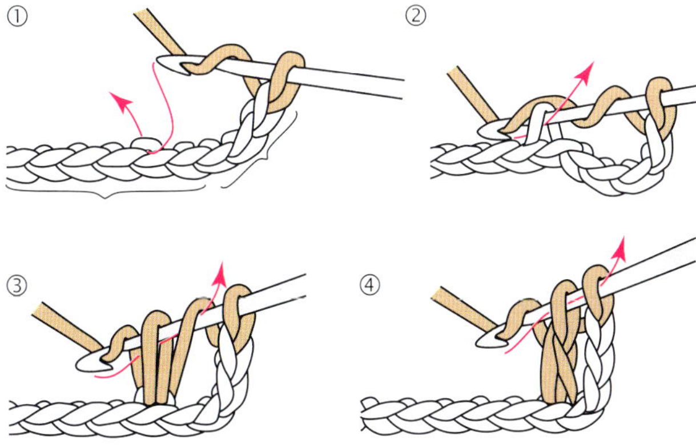

HALF DOUBLE CROCHET

1. Yarn round hook and insert the hook into the back of the chain stitch as shown by the arrow.
2. Yarn round hook, then draw through the loop, yarn round hook again and draw through all the loops on the hook.

Repeat Steps 1 and 2 as many times as required. On following rows, work into the two strands at the top of each stitch instead of the back of the foundation chain.

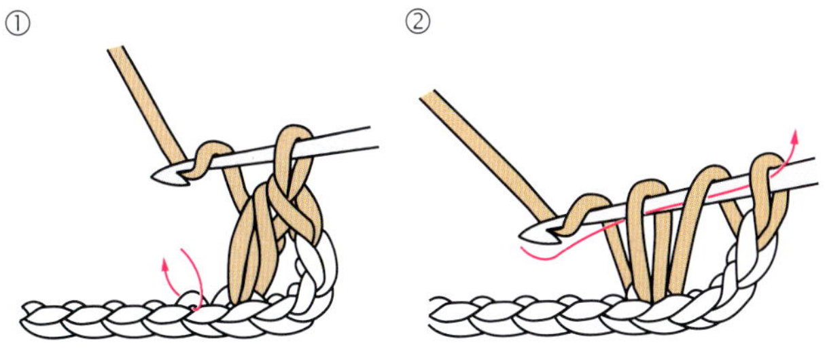

TREBLE CROCHET

1. Yarn round hook, then insert the hook into the back of the chain as shown by the arrow.
2. Yarn round hook, then draw through the loop, yarn round hook again and draw through two loops.
3. Yarn round hook, then draw through two loops.
4. Yarn round hook, then draw through the two remaining loops on the hook.

Repeat Steps 1–4 as many times as required. On following rows, work into the two strands at the top of each stitch instead of the back of the foundation chain.

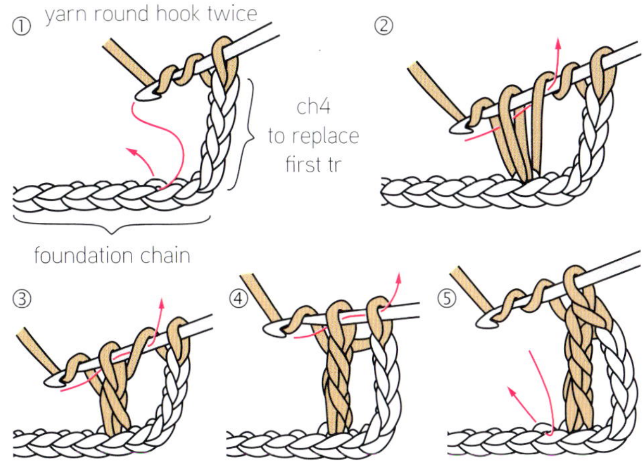

SINGLE CROCHET INCREASE

1. Work one single crochet before inserting the hook into the same stitch that you have just worked, then yarn round hook.
2. Draw through the stitch, yarn round hook and draw through the two loops on the hook.
3. Your increase is complete.

Note: for half double, double, or treble increases, the principle is the same: you simply work two half doubles, two doubles, or two trebles into the same stitch.

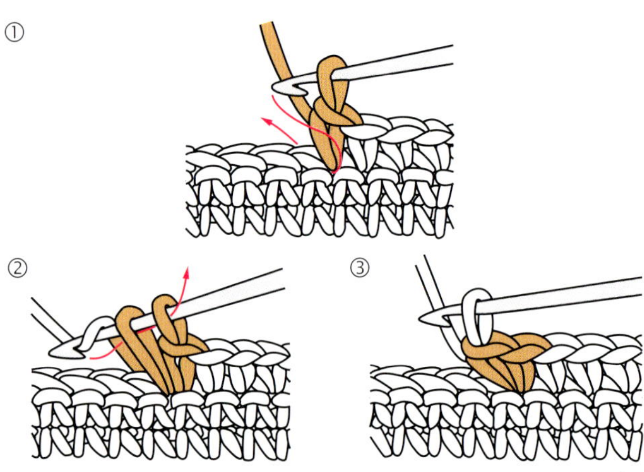

3 HALF DOUBLE CROCHET BOBBLE

1. Yarn round hook, then insert the hook into the stitch marked by arrow 1, yarn round hook and draw through the stitch.
2. [Yarn round hook, insert the hook into the same stitch, yarn over and draw back through the stitch] twice (arrows 2 and 3). You have seven loops on the hook (three incomplete half double crochet stitches).
3. Yarn round hook and draw through all the loops on the hook.

Note: for two half double crochet bobbles (2hdc-bo) work Step 2 without repeating sts in square brackets so you only have two incomplete half double crochet stitches.

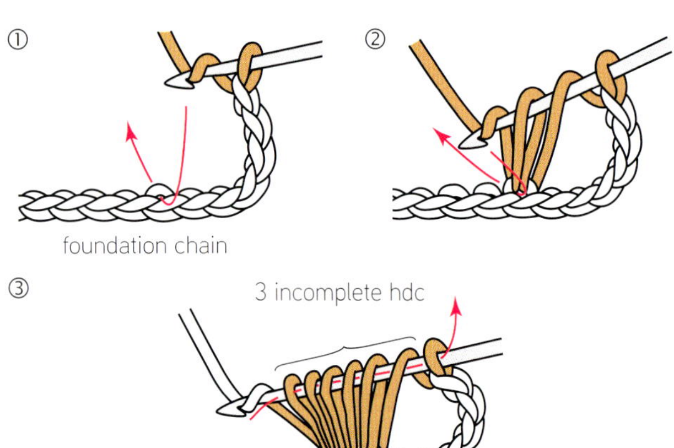

SINGLE CROCHET INVISIBLE DECREASE

1. Insert the hook into the front loop of a stitch, then immediately insert it into the front loop of the next stitch. You have three loops on the hook.
2. Yarn round hook, then draw through the first two loops on the hook.
3. Yarn round hook, then draw through the two remaining loops on the hook.

The invisible decrease is complete.

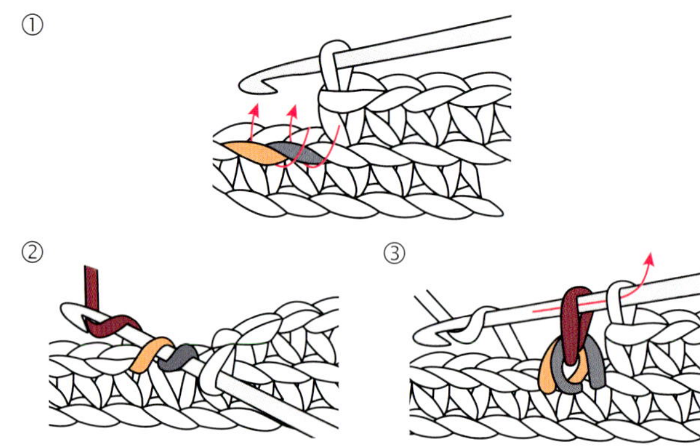

FRONT LOOP AND BACK LOOP ONLY

The top part of a stitch consists of two loops, one at the front towards you (= the front loop ①) and one at the back (= back loop ②).

If required, only work into the front loop or the back loop of the stitch, without changing anything else about how you work the stitch.

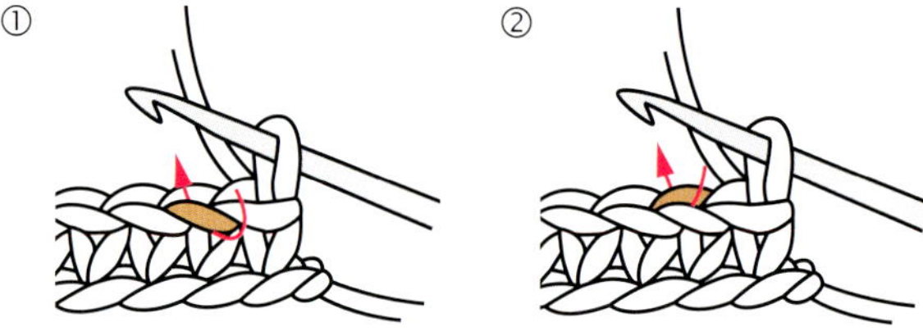

INVISIBLE FINISH

1. Complete the last stitch, cut the yarn and draw it through this stitch.
2. Skip one stitch and take the yarn (using a yarn needle) under both loops of the next stitch.
3. Bring the needle back out in the last stitch.

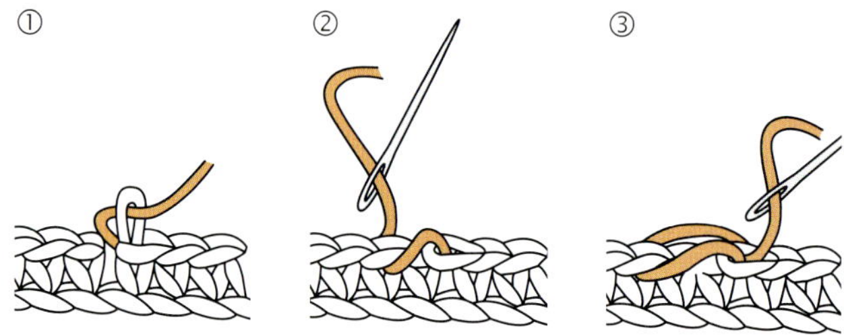

STARTING WORK IN AN OVAL

Some pieces start by working an oval around a foundation chain.
Work the required number of chain stitches (= foundation chain).

1. Skip the first chain stitch from the hook, then work one single crochet into the next chain stitch.
2. Work the subsequent single crochets into each chain stitch of the foundation chain, in accordance with the instructions, bearing in mind that in general several single crochets are worked into the last chain stitch of the foundation chain.
3. Turn the work to move on to the other side of the foundation chain.

Note: there is only one loop available under which to insert the hook.

Work single crochets into each chain stitch. When you reach the end, the last stitch is located next to the very first stitch.

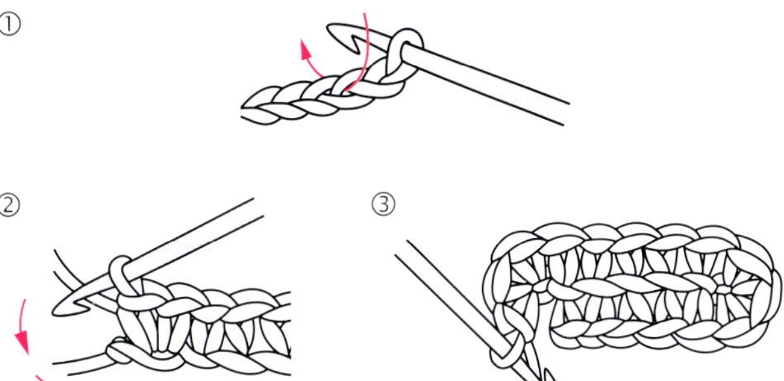

CHANGING COLOR

1. Start working the stitch where you want to change color, but do not finish it (two loops still remain on the hook)
2. Yarn round hook using the new color, then draw it through the two remaining loops on the hook.

Note: for work where there are several alternating colors (stripes), always change color on the last yarn round hook of the round in question.

Leave the unused yarn waiting on the wrong side of the work as you continue in the new color, then pick up the waiting yarn again on the next round.

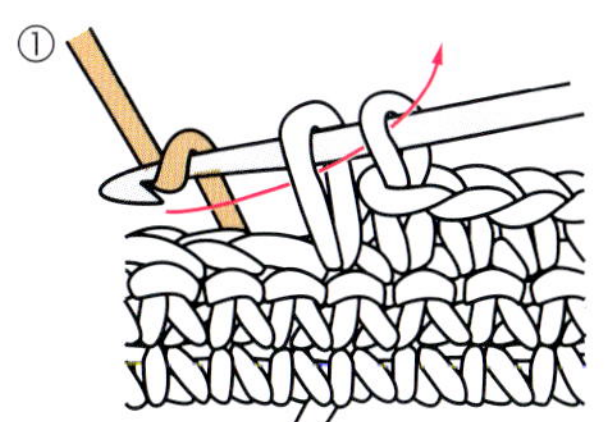

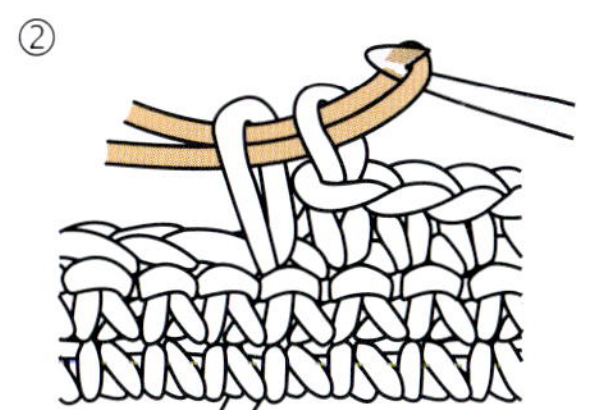

X-SHAPED SINGLE CROCHET

1. Insert the hook into the stitch, wrap the yarn under the hook.
2. Draw the yarn through the stitch, wrap the yarn over the hook, and draw through both loops.

This gives a denser finish, and the stitches are better defined.

Note : the final result is a little smaller, given the same size yarn and hook, than classic V-shaped single crochets.

If you inserted the hook into the stitch, then you are drawing it back through the stitch (even if it looks like a loop).

WORKING IN SPIRAL ROUNDS

After you have made a magic ring, carry on working in rounds (generally in single crochet) around this ring. The rounds are worked one after the other without stopping (like an endless screw thread).

Embroidery Basics

BACK STITCH

Worked from right to left.
Bring out the floss at 1. Insert the needle again at 2, then bring it out again at 3. Repeat these steps, forming very even stitches.

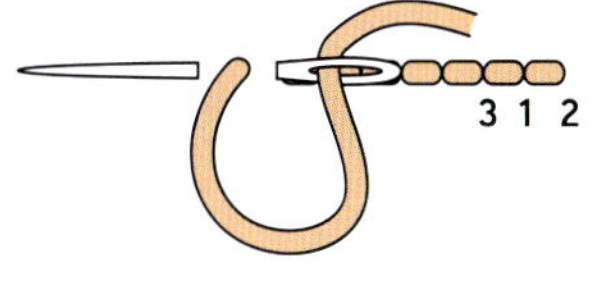

FRENCH KNOT

1. Bring out the floss at 1. Wrap it two or three times around the needle, pinching it between the thumb and forefinger of your left hand.
2. Pull the needle through gently, then reinsert it at 2, just next to point 1.

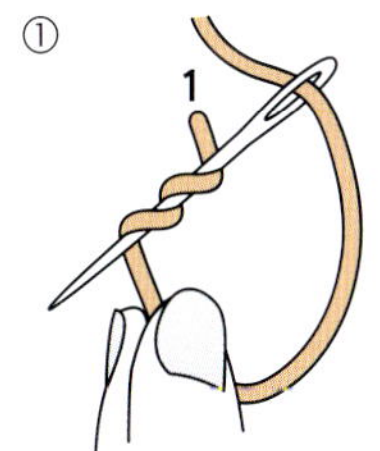

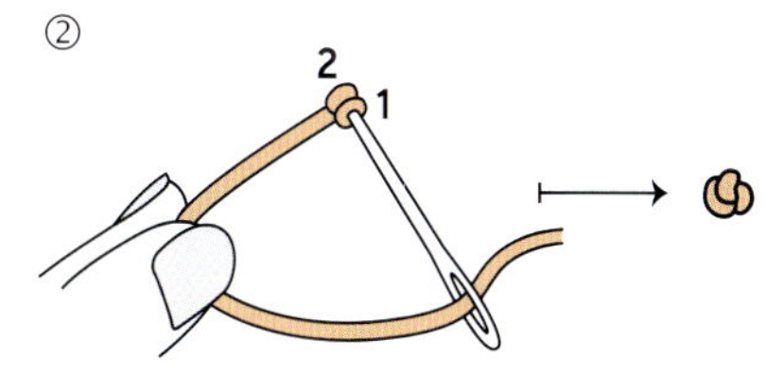

Abbreviations

2hdc-bo : 2hdc bobble
3sc-bo : 3sc bobble
3hdc-bo : 3hdc bobble
BLO : work into the back loop only of the previous round/row
ch : chain
dc : double crochet
dc-dec : 2dc together
dc-inc : 2dc in same st/sp
dec : sc invisible decrease
FLO : work into the front loop only of the previous round/row
hdc : half double crochet
hdc-dec : 2hdc together
hdc-inc : 2hdc in same st/sp
inc : 2sc in same st/sp
MR : magic ring
st(s) : stitch(es)
sc : single crochet
sk : skip
slst(s) : slip stitch(es)
sp : space
tr : treble crochet
tr-inc : 2tr in same st/sp

[...] : a group of stitches to be repeated or worked in a specific place (e.g. leg 1).

(...) : in stitch instructions, work the action described in brackets into one stitch. At the end of a row, round brackets contain stitch counts.

Difficulty: ● ● ○ intermediate ● ● ● advanced

Techniques

Always use X-shaped stitches and joined rounds, unless stated otherwise.

Working in Joined Rounds

JOINING A ROUND

At the end of the round, pull up the loop of the last stitch (1). Insert the hook into the first stitch of the round, from wrong side to right side (2).
Pick up the loop with the hook (3) and draw it through the first stitch of the round (4). This creates one slip stitch on the wrong side.

Note: it is equally possible to work a regular slip stitch to join a round, but it will be more visible.

STARTING A ROUND

Chain 1, then make the first stitch of the round, inserting the hook into the stitch where the slip stitch joined the previous round (5, 6).

Note: the slip stitches at the end of the round and the chains at the start of the round are not included in stitch counts.

Working into a Foundation Chain

On the right side of a chain, there are V-shaped stitches (7). The wrong side of a chain is marked by little bumps (8). You need to work into these bumps (9). This gives a more attractive end look (10).

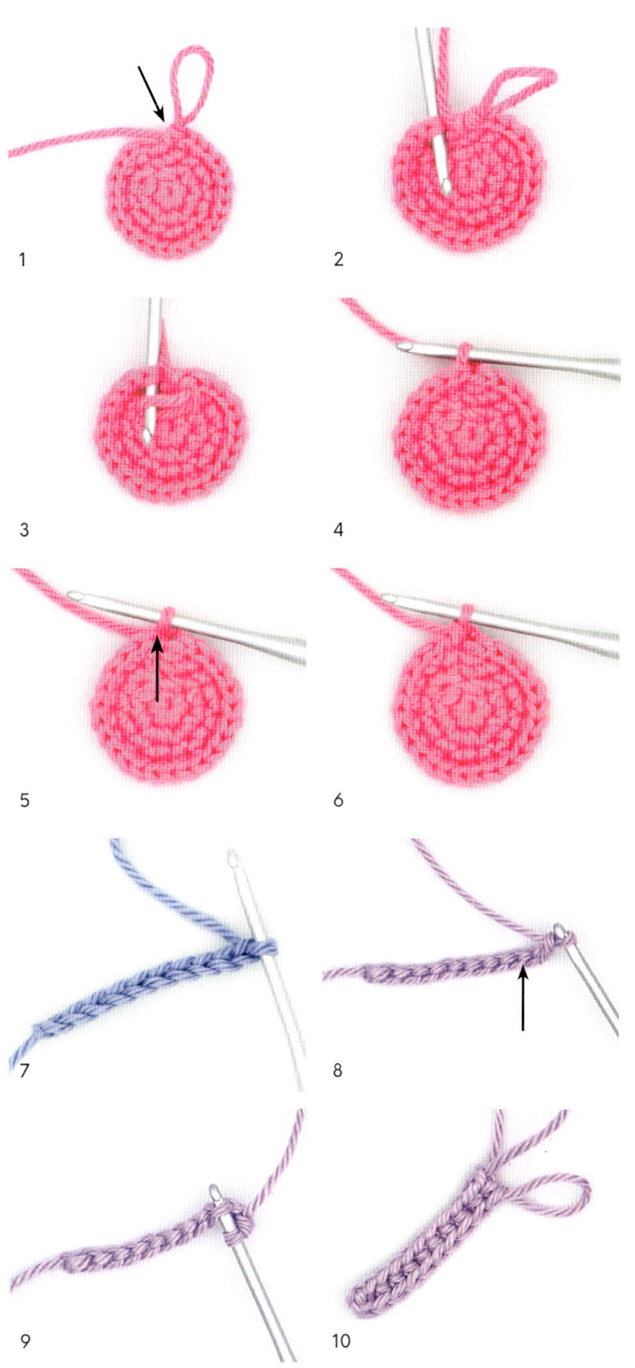

Joining New Yarn

Draw the new yarn through the stitch (11, 12). Start working the required stitches into the next stitch (13). To join the round, the last stitch should be worked in the same stitch through which the yarn was drawn at the start (14). Fasten off and weave in the tail (15).

Finishing a Spherical Piece

Once the piece is finished, cut the yarn. Thread the tail from outside to inside through the front loops of all the stitches (16). Pull on the yarn to close the hole and fasten off, passing it down through the center of the hole (17, 18).

3-Single Crochet Bobble (3sc-bo)

Insert the hook into the stitch (19). Yarn round hook, then draw through the stitch (20). Yarn round hook again and draw the yarn through only one loop on the hook. There are now two loops on the hook (21). Insert the hook into the same stitch again and repeat the process twice more. There are now four loops on the hook (22). Yarn round hook and draw the yarn through the four loops (23).

Joining the Legs

All the dolls begin with the legs, which are worked separately, then joined just before crocheting the body. In this book, there are two different ways of joining the legs (Diagrams 1 and 2).

Diagram 1

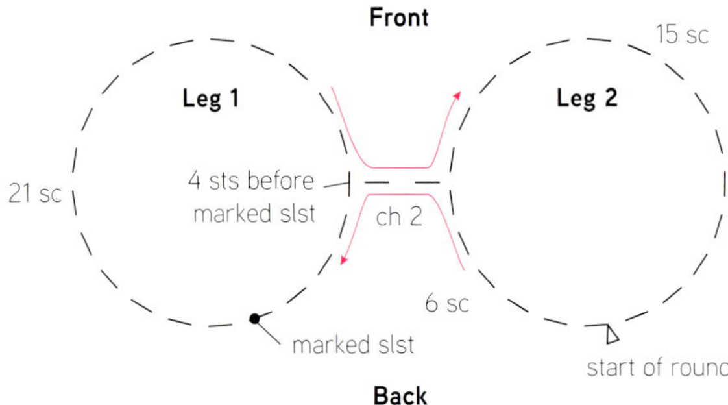

Diagram 2

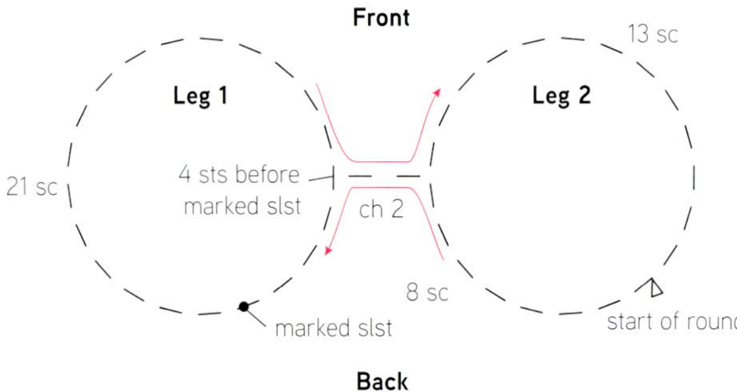

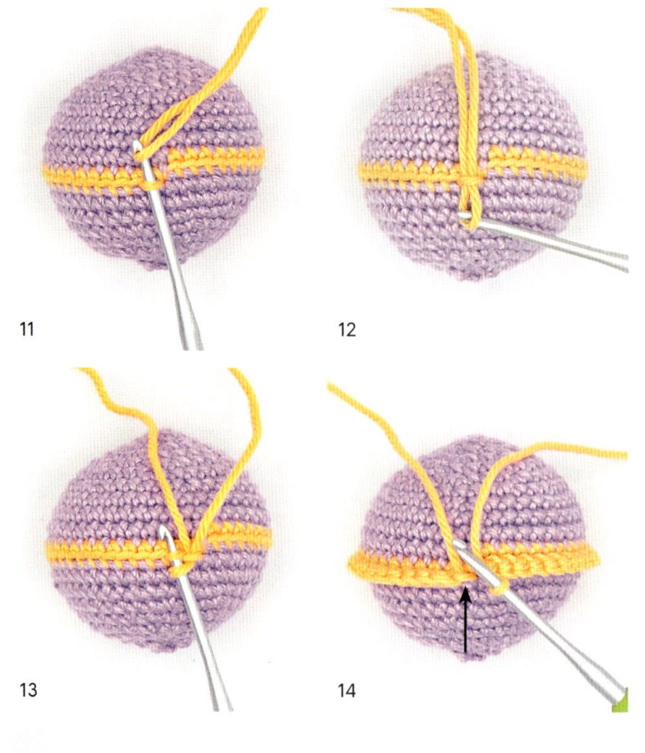

11 12 13 14

15

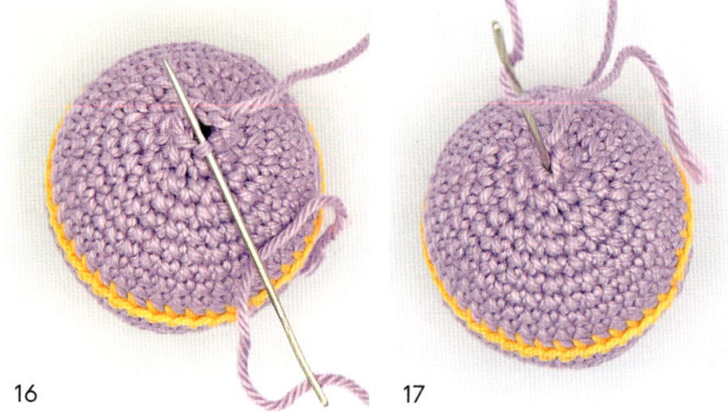

16 17

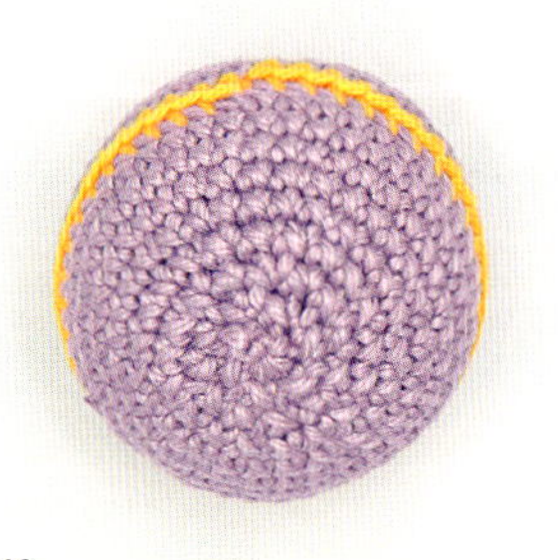

18

19

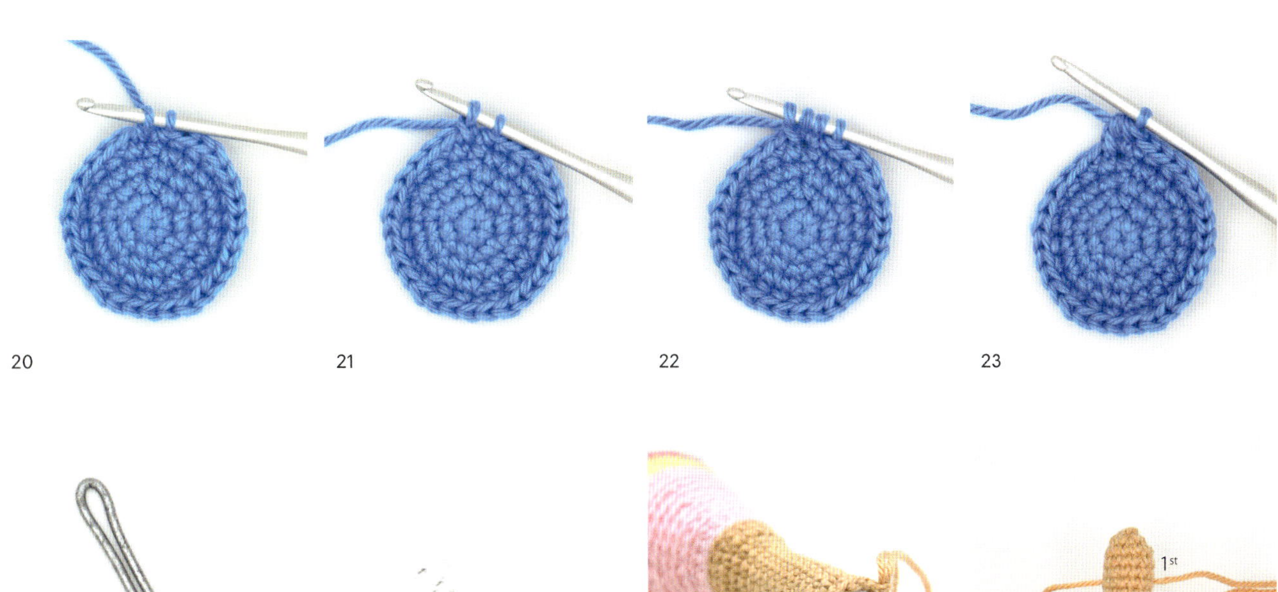

20 21 22 23

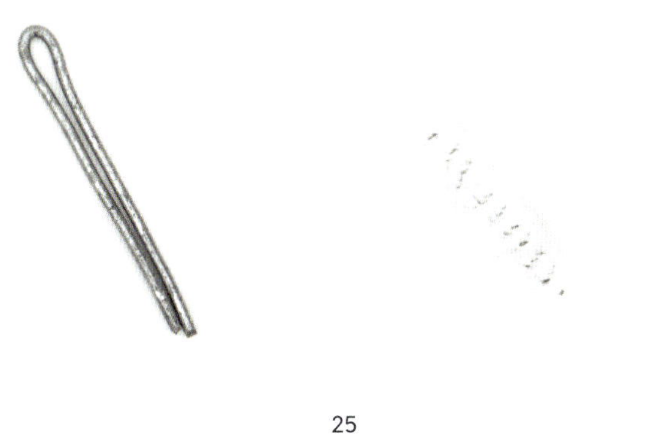

24 25 26 27

Strengthening the Neck

Cut a 3¼in (8cm) length of 0.06in (1.5mm) aluminum wire and fold it in half (24). Wrap a chenille stem around the length of wire (25) then insert into the neck (26).

Attaching the Head

Use the color given in the instructions.

Thread three strands of yarn through the neck (27).
Thread both ends of the first strand up through the head, bringing them out in the center of the magic ring at the top of the head (28).
Do the same with the second and third strands (29).
Pull on all the strands so the neck sits snugly inside the head. Leave visible the number of rounds specified in the instructions (30).
Knot the first strand and weave it into the head. Do the same with the second and third strands.
The head is now in place and is movable.

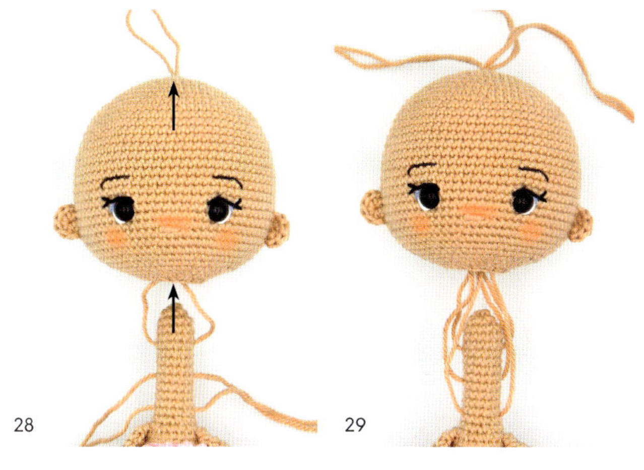

28 29

30

Standard Parts

In this book, the soles of the shoes and the bodies of the companions (except for Mitsuki) are identical for all models and are explained in this chapter.

Soles of the Shoes (make 2)

Note: work the soles in ovals around a foundation chain.

Using the color given in the instructions, ch5, and start in the second ch from hook.
Round 1: inc, 2 sc, 4 sc into last ch to pass to other side of foundation chain, 3 sc. (11 sts)
Round 2: inc twice, 2 sc, inc 4 times, 2 sc, inc. (18 sts)
Round 3: [1 sc, inc] twice, 2 sc, [1 sc, inc] 4 times, 3 sc, inc. (25 sts)
Cut the yarn and work an invisible finish.
Mark the finishing stitch. Work another identical sole, but without marking the finishing stitch *(1)*.
Lay one piece on top of the other, WS together, aligning the sts.
Taking the 2 pieces together, join the color given in the instructions into the finishing stitch and the stitch facing it *(2)*, and work as follows:
Round 1: 25 slst. (25 sts)
Fasten off and weave in ends. Then continue the shoes according to the instructions given for the different projects.

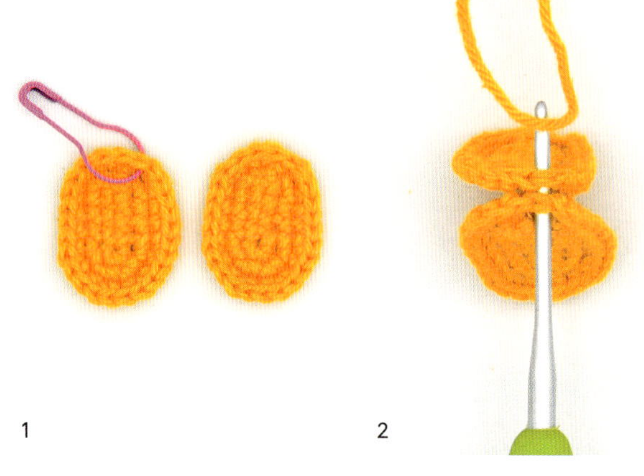
1 2

The Little Companions

BIG BODY

Using the color given in the instructions, make MR, and crochet in joined rounds.
Round 1: 6 sc into MR, slst to join. (6 sts)
Round 2: ch1, inc in each st around, slst to join. (12 sts)
Round 3: ch1, [1 sc, inc] 6 times, slst to join. (18 sts)
Round 4: ch1, [1 sc, inc, 1 sc] 6 times, slst to join. (24 sts)
Round 5: ch1, 1 sc in each st around, slst to join.
Round 6: ch1, [7 sc, inc] 3 times, slst to join. (27 sts)
Round 7: ch1, 1 sc in each st around, slst to join.
Round 8: ch1, [4 sc, inc, 4 sc] 3 times, slst to join. (30 sts)
Round 9: ch1, 1 sc in each st around, slst to join.
Round 10: ch1, [9 sc, inc] 3 times, slst to join. (33 sts)
Round 11: ch1, 1 sc in each st around, slst to join.
Round 12: ch1, [5 sc, inc, 5 sc] 3 times, slst to join. (36 sts)
Round 13: ch1, 1 sc in each st around, slst to join.
Round 14: ch1, [11 sc, inc] 3 times, slst to join. (39 sts)
Round 15: ch1, 1 sc in each st around, slst to join.
Round 16: ch1, [6 sc, inc, 6 sc] 3 times, slst to join. (42 sts)
Round 17: ch1, 1 sc in each st around, slst to join.
Round 18: ch1, [13 sc, inc] 3 times, slst to join. (45 sts)
Round 19: ch1, 1 sc in each st around, slst to join.
Round 20: ch1, [7 sc, inc, 7 sc] 3 times, slst to join. (48 sts)
Rounds 21 and 22 (2 rounds): ch1, 1 sc in each st around, slst to join.
Round 23: ch1, [6 sc, dec] 6 times, slst to join. (42 sts)
Round 24: ch1, [5 sc, dec] 6 times, slst BLO to join. (36 sts)
Round 25: ch1, [4 sc BLO, dec BLO] 6 times, slst to join. (30 sts)
Round 26: ch1, [3 sc, dec] 6 times, slst to join. (24 sts)
Round 27: ch1, [2 sc, dec] 6 times, slst to join. (18 sts)
Stuff.
Round 28: ch1, [1 sc, dec] 6 times, slst to join. (12 sts)
Round 29: ch1, dec 6 times, slst to join. (6 sts)
Cut the yarn and fasten off *(3)*.
Using the Black floss, embroider the eyes on Round 10, leaving a gap of 4 sts between them *(4)*.
Using the White floss, embroider 1 st in each eye *(5)*.

MEDIUM-SIZED BODY

Using the color given in the instructions, make MR, and crochet in joined rounds.
Round 1: 6 sc into MR, slst to join. (6 sts)
Round 2: ch1, inc in each st around, slst to join. (12 sts)
Round 3: ch1, [1 sc, inc] 6 times, slst to join. (18 sts)
Round 4: ch1, [1 sc, inc, 1 sc] 6 times, slst to join. (24 sts)
Round 5: ch1, 1 sc in each st around, slst to join.
Round 6: ch1, [7 sc, inc] 3 times, slst to join. (27 sts)
Round 7: ch1, 1 sc in each st around, slst to join.
Round 8: ch1, [4 sc, inc, 4 sc] 3 times, slst to join. (30 sts)
Round 9: ch1, 1 sc in each st around, slst to join.
Round 10: ch1, [9 sc, inc] 3 times, slst to join. (33 sts)
Round 11: ch1, 1 sc in each st around, slst to join.
Round 12: ch1, [5 sc, inc, 5 sc] 3 times, slst to join. (36 sts)
Round 13: ch1, 1 sc in each st around, slst to join.
Round 14: ch1, [11 sc, inc] 3 times, slst to join. (39 sts)
Round 15: ch1, 1 sc in each st around, slst to join.
Round 16: ch1, [6 sc, inc, 6 sc] 3 times, slst to join. (42 sts)
Rounds 17 and 18 (2 rounds): ch1, 1 sc in each st around, slst to join.
Round 19: ch1, [5 sc, dec] 6 times, slst to join. (36 sts)
Round 20: ch1, [4 sc, dec] 6 times, slst BLO to join. (30 sts)
Round 21: ch1, [3 sc BLO, dec BLO] 6 times, slst to join. (24 sts)
Round 22: ch1, [2 sc, dec] 6 times, slst to join. (18 sts)
Stuff.
Round 23: ch1, [1 sc, dec] 6 times, slst to join. (12 sts)
Round 24: ch1, dec, slst to join. (6 sts)
Cut the yarn and fasten off *(3)*.
Using the Black floss, embroider the eyes on Round 8, leaving a gap of 4 sts between them *(4)*.
Using the White floss, embroider 1 st in each eye *(5)*.

3

4

5

SMALL BODY

Using the color given in the instructions, make MR, and crochet in joined rounds.
Round 1: 6 sc into MR, slst to join. (6 sts)
Round 2: ch1, inc in each st around, slst to join. (12 sts)
Round 3: ch1, [1 sc, inc] 6 times, slst to join. (18 sts)
Round 4: ch1, [1 sc, inc, 1 sc] 6 times, slst to join. (24 sts)
Round 5: ch1, 1 sc in each st around, slst to join.
Round 6: ch1, [7 sc, inc] 3 times, slst to join. (27 sts)
Round 7: ch1, 1 sc in each st around, slst to join.
Round 8: ch1, [4 sc, inc, 4 sc] 3 times, slst to join. (30 sts)
Round 9: ch1, 1 sc in each st around, slst to join.
Round 10: ch1, [9 sc, inc] 3 times, slst to join. (33 sts)
Round 11: ch1, 1 sc in each st around, slst to join.
Round 12: ch1, [5 sc, inc, 5 sc] 3 times, slst to join. (36 sts)
Rounds 13 and 14 (2 rounds): ch1, 1 sc in each st around, slst to join.
Round 15: ch1, [4 sc, dec] 6 times, slst to join. (30 sts)
Round 16: ch1, [3 sc, dec] 6 times, slst BLO to join. (24 sts)
Round 17: ch1, [2 sc BLO, dec BLO] 6 times, slst to join. (18 sts)
Stuff.
Round 18: ch1, [1 sc, dec] 6 times, slst to join. (12 sts)
Round 19: ch1, dec 6 times, slst to join. (6 sts)
Cut the yarn and fasten off *(3)*.
Using the Black floss, embroider the eyes on Round 8, leaving a gap of 4 sts between them *(4)*.
Using the White floss, embroider 1 st in each eye *(5)*.

The Characters

A big foodie, Aya loves lollipops and colorful candies. She and her little companions have fun sliding across rainbows, scattering pretty treats.

Finished Size

Aya: approx 9½in (24cm) tall
Companions: between 1¾in (4.5cm) and 2¾in (7cm) tall

Note:
Size may vary depending on your gauge (tension) and the yarn used

Tools and Materials

Yarn and Colors Must-Have yarn in the following colors:

US 4 (2.00mm) crochet hook
Fiberfill stuffing
2 x 7mm safety eyes
Basic tool kit
(see Materials)

Instructions

Note: always use X-shaped stitches and joined rounds, unless stated otherwise.

Legs (make 2)

Using Blossom, make MR.
Round 1: 6 sc into MR, slst to join. (6 sts)
Round 2: ch1, inc in each st around, slst to join. (12 sts)
Round 3: ch1, [1 sc, inc] 6 times, slst to join. (18 sts)
Rounds 4 and 5 (2 rounds): ch1, 1 sc in each st around, slst to join.
Round 6: ch1, 6 sc, dec 3 times, 6 sc, slst to join. (15 sts)
Round 7: ch1, 5 sc, dec, 1 sc, dec, 5 sc, slst to join. (13 sts)
Round 8: ch1, 1 sc in each st around, slst BLO to join.
Rounds 9 and 10 (2 rounds): ch1, 1 sc BLO of each st around, slst BLO to join.
Round 11: ch1, 1 sc BLO of each st around, change to Marble, slst BLO to join.
Round 12: ch1, 1 sc BLO of each st around, slst to join. (13 sts)
Round 13: ch1, 2 sc, inc, 7 sc, inc, 2 sc, slst to join. (15 sts)
Rounds 14–16 (3 rounds): ch1, 1 sc in each st around, slst to join.
Round 17: ch1, 2 sc, dec, 7 sc, dec, 2 sc, slst to join. (13 sts)
Round 18: ch1, 2 sc, inc, 7 sc, inc, 2 sc, slst to join. (15 sts)
Stuff the foot.
Round 19: ch1, 3 sc, inc, 7 sc, inc, 3 sc, slst to join. (17 sts)
Round 20: ch1, 1 sc in each st around, change to Limestone.

Round 21: slst BLO of each st around.
Round 22: 4 sc BLO, inc BLO, 7 sc BLO, inc BLO, 4 sc BLO, slst to join. (19 sts)
Round 23: ch1, 1 sc in each st around, slst to join.
Round 24: ch1, 5 sc, inc, 7 sc, inc, 5 sc, slst to join. (21 sts)
Round 25: ch1, 1 sc in each st around, slst to join.
Round 26: ch1, 1 sc in each st around, change to Marble, slst to join.
Round 27: ch1, 1 sc in each st around, slst to join.
Round 28: ch1, 1 sc in each st around, slst on RS.
Mark last slst.
Leg 1: fasten off and weave in ends.
Stuff leg firmly.
Join Blossom yarn to FLO of last st of Round 8 *(1)*, [ch4, slst FLO] in all sts of Rounds 8–11 *(2)*.
Fasten off and weave in ends. Set aside.
Leg 2: repeat steps as for leg 1, but at end, work last slst on WS. Stuff leg firmly. Do not mark last slst, do not cut yarn, but continue as follows:

1 2

Body

Note: see Diagram I, Techniques: Joining the Legs.

Round 29: ch1, 6 sc into leg 2, ch2, then 1 sc into fourth st before marked slst, 3 sc, 1 sc into same st as marked slst, 16 sc on leg 1, 2 sc into 2 ch and 15 sc into remaining sts of leg 2, slst to join. (46 sts)
Round 30: ch1, 6 sc into leg 2, 2 sc in opposite side of ch2, then dec, 21 sc on leg 1 and dec, 13 sc on remaining sts of leg 2, slst to join. (44 sts)

Note: stuff as you go along.

Rounds 31–35 (5 rounds): ch1, 1 sc in each st around, slst to join.
Round 36: ch1, 22 sc, dec, 10 sc, dec, 8 sc, slst to join. (42 sts)
Round 37: ch1, 1 sc in each st around, change to Peony Pink, slst to join.
Round 38: ch1, 21 sc, dec, 10 sc, dec, 7 sc, change to Vanilla, slst BLO. (40 sts)
Round 39: ch1, 1 sc BLO of each st around, slst to join.
Round 40: ch1, [8 sc, dec] 4 times, slst to join. (36 sts)
Round 41: ch1, 1 sc in each st around, change to Blossom.
Round 42: slst BLO of each st around.
Round 43: ch1, 1 sc BLO of each st around, slst to join.
Round 44: ch1, [7 sc, dec] 4 times, slst BLO to join. (32 sts)
Round 45: ch1, 1 sc BLO of each st around, slst BLO to join.
Round 46: ch1, [6 sc BLO, dec BLO] 4 times, slst BLO to join. (28 sts)
Round 47: ch1, 1 sc BLO of each st around, slst BLO to join.
Round 48: ch1, [5 sc BLO, dec BLO] 4 times, slst BLO to join. (24 sts)
Round 49: ch1, 1 sc BLO of each st around, slst BLO to join.
Round 50: ch1, 11 sc BLO, dec BLO, 9 sc BLO, dec BLO, slst BLO to join. (22 sts)
Round 51: ch1, 1 sc BLO of each st around, slst to join.

Round 52: ch1, 10 sc, dec, 8 sc, dec, 5 sc, then start next round in middle of back. (20 sts)
Change to Limestone.
Round 53: slst BLO of each st around.
Round 54: ch1, 1 sc BLO of each st around, slst to join.
Round 55: ch1, [3 sc, dec] 4 times, slst to join. (16 sts)
Round 56: ch1, [3 sc, dec] twice, 4 sc, dec, slst to join. (13 sts)
Rounds 57–67 (11 rounds): ch1, 1 sc in each st around, slst to join.
Round 68: ch1, 5 sc, dec, 6 sc, slst to join. (12 sts)

Note: strengthen the neck (see Techniques: Strengthening the Neck).

Round 69: ch1, dec, slst to join. (6 sts)
Cut the yarn and fasten off (3).
Join Blossom yarn in FLO of middle of back of Round 44 (4) and work [ch4, 1 sc FLO] in all sts on rounds 44–50 (5, 6).
Fasten off and weave in ends.

Skirt

Holding the body neck down, join Peony Pink yarn to 1 FLO on back of Round 38. (7).
Round 1: [ch3, 1 sc FLO] 40 times, slst into first ch sp. (40 sc, 40 ch3-sp)
Rounds 2 and 3 (2 rounds): ch3, 1 sc into first ch3-sp, [ch3, 1 sc into next ch3-sp) 39 times, 1 sc into first ch3-sp.
Round 4: ch1, inc into first ch3-sp, [inc into next ch3-sp] 39 times, slst to join. (80 sts)
Round 5: ch1, [3 sc, dec] 16 times, slst BLO. (64 sts)
Round 6: [ch3, 1 sc BLO] 64 times, slst into first ch3-sp. (64 sc, 64 ch3-sp)
Rounds 7 and 8 (2 rounds): ch3, 1 sc into first ch3-sp, [ch3, 1 sc into next ch3-sp] 63 times, slst into first ch-sp.
Round 9: ch3, 1 sc into first ch3-sp, [ch3, 1 sc into next ch3-sp] 63 times, change to Opaline Glass, slst into first ch3-sp.
Round 10: [ch3, slst into first ch3-sp, ch3, slst into same ch3-sp], [ch3, slst into next ch3-sp, ch3, slst into same ch3-sp] 63 times, slst (128 ch3-sp).
Fasten off and weave in ends (8).

Arms (make 2)

Using Mustard, make MR.
Round 1: 6 sc into MR, slst to join. (6 sts)
Round 2: ch1, [1 sc, inc] 3 times, slst to join. (9 sts)
Round 3: ch1, [2 sc, inc] 3 times, slst to join. (12 sts)
Round 4: ch1, 1 sc in each st around, slst to join.
Round 5: ch1, 5 sc, dec, 5 sc, slst to join. (11 sts)
Round 6: ch1, 5 sc, 1 3sc-bo (= thumb), 5 sc, slst to join.

3

4

5

6

7

8

Round 7: ch1, 5 sc, dec, 2 sc, dec, slst to join. (9 sts)
Round 8: ch1, 1 sc in each st around, change to Blossom, slst to join.
Round 9: ch1, 5 sc, dec, 2 sc, slst BLO to join.
Stuff hand firmly.
Round 10: ch1, 1 sc BLO of each st around, change to Limestone, slst BLO to join.
Round 11: ch1, 1 sc BLO of each st around, slst to join.
Rounds 12–18 (7 rounds): ch1, 1 sc in each st around, slst to join.
Round 19: ch1, 4 sc, dec, 2 sc, slst to join.
Rounds 20–23 (4 rounds): ch1, 1 sc in each st around, slst to join.
Round 24: ch1, 1 sc in each st around, slst on RS to join.
Stuff the arms lightly halfway.
Flatten out the opening then work 3 sc through both thicknesses at the same time to close.
Fasten off and cut, leaving enough yarn for sewing to body.
Join Blossom yarn to FLO of last st of Round 9 *(9)*, [ch4, 1 slst FLO] in all sts in Rounds 9 and 10. Fasten off and weave in ends *(10)*.
Sew one arm on to each side of the body between Rounds 53 and 54, ensuring that the thumbs are positioned at the front *(11, 12)*.

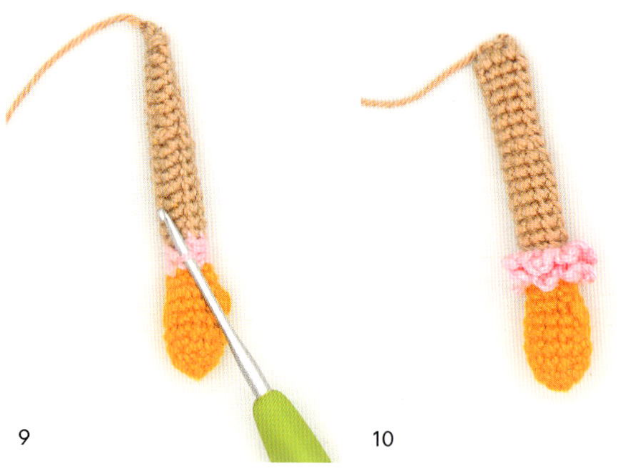
9 10

11

12

Head

Using Limestone, make MR.
Round 1: 6 sc into MR, slst to join. (6 sts)
Round 2: ch1, inc in each st around, slst to join. (12 sts)
Round 3: ch1, [1 sc, inc] 6 times, slst to join. (18 sts)
Round 4: ch1, [1 sc, inc, 1 sc] 6 times, slst to join. (24 sts)
Round 5: ch1, [3 sc, inc] 6 times, slst to join. (30 sts)
Round 6: ch1, [2 sc, inc, 2 sc] 6 times, slst to join. (36 sts)
Round 7: ch1, [5 sc, inc] 6 times, slst to join. (42 sts)
Round 8: ch1, [3 sc, inc, 3 sc] 6 times, slst to join. (48 sts)
Round 9: ch1, [7 sc, inc] 6 times, slst to join. (54 sts)
Round 10: ch1, [4 sc, inc, 4 sc] 6 times, slst to join. (60 sts)
Round 11: ch1, 1 sc in each st around, slst to join.
Round 12: ch1, [9 sc, inc] 6 times, slst to join. (66 sts)
Round 13: ch1, 1 sc in each st around, slst to join.
Round 14: ch1, 16 sc, inc, 32 sc, inc, 16 sc, slst to join. (68 sts)
Rounds 15–23 (9 rounds): ch1, 1 sc in each st around, slst to join.
Round 24: ch1, 28 sc, ch1, sk 1 st, 10 sc, ch1, sk 1 st, 28 sc, slst to join.
Round 25: ch1, 28 sc, 1 sc into ch, 10 sc, 1 sc into ch, 28 sc, slst to join.
Round 26: ch1, 16 sc, dec, 32 sc, dec, 16 sc, slst to join. (66 sts)
Round 27: ch1, 1 sc in each st around, slst to join.
Round 28: ch1, 15 sc, dec, 32 sc, dec, 15 sc, slst to join. (64 sts)
Insert the eyes into the holes formed by the skipped sts in Round 24.
Round 29: ch1, [14 sc, dec] 4 times, slst to join. (60 sts)

13

14

15

Round 30: ch1, [4 sc, dec, 4 sc] 6 times, slst to join. (54 sts)
Round 31: ch1, [7 sc, dec] 6 times, slst to join. (48 sts)
Round 32: ch1, [4 sc, dec] 8 times, slst to join. (40 sts)
Round 33: ch1, [3 sc, dec] 8 times, slst to join. (32 sts)
Start to stuff.
Round 34: ch1, [2 sc, dec] 8 times, slst to join. (24 sts)
Round 35: ch1, [1 sc, dec] 8 times, slst BLO to join. (16 sts)
Round 36: ch1, 1 sc BLO of each st around, slst to join.
Rounds 37–41 (5 rounds): ch1, 1 sc in each st around, slst to join.
Fasten off and weave in ends. Complete the stuffing.
Push Rounds 36–41 inside the head *(13)*.
Using White floss, embroider the whites of the eyes *(14)*, then add a touch of Blue floss to the sides of the eyes *(15)*.
Using Black floss, embroider the black above the eyes, and finish by embroidering the eyelashes *(16, 17)*.
Using the Brown floss, embroider the eyebrows between Rounds 20 and 22 *(18)*.
Using Limestone, embroider the nose between Rounds 26 and 27 *(19)*.
Use a brush and some blush to add a little color to the cheeks and above the nose *(20)*.

Note: the circumference of the head once stuffed is approximately 7½in (19cm).

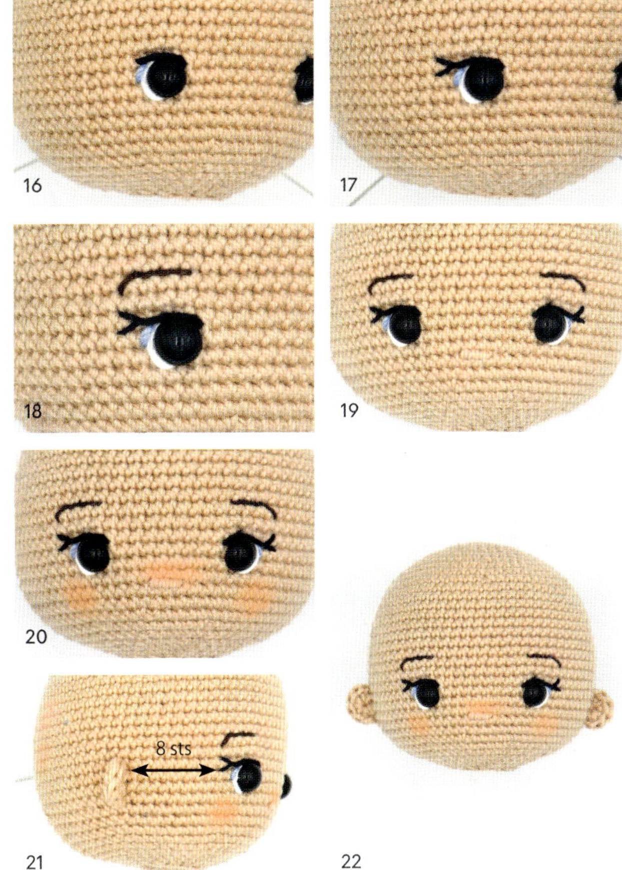

EARS (MAKE 2)

Using Limestone, make MR.
Round 1: 1 sc, 4 hdc, 1 sc into MR. (6 sts)
Fasten off, leaving sufficient yarn for sewing to head.
Sew one ear to each side of the head between Rounds 23 and 27, leaving a gap of 8 sts between ear and eye *(21, 22)*.

ATTACH THE HEAD

Using Limestone, attach the head according to instructions in Techniques: Attaching the Head. Leave 5 rounds in Limestone visible.

Hair

PART 1

Using Vanilla, make MR.
Round 1: 6 sc into MR, slst to join. (6 sts)
Round 2: ch1, inc in each st around, slst FLO to join. (12 sts)
Round 3: ch1, [1 sc FLO, inc FLO] 6 times, slst FLO to join. (18 sts)
Round 4: ch1, [1 sc FLO, inc FLO, 1 sc FLO] 6 times, slst to join. (24 sts)
Round 5: ch1, [3 sc, inc] 6 times, slst to join. (30 sts)
Do not cut the yarn and continue with the strands of hair.

Note: it is the WS of the strands of hair that will be visible.

Strand 1: ch60, and starting in second ch from hook: slst, 1 sc, 57 hdc, change to Opaline Glass, slst into next st of Round 5.
Strand 2: ch60, and starting in second ch from hook: slst, 1 sc, 57 hdc, change to Salmon, slst into next st of Round 5.
Strand 3: ch60, and starting in second ch from hook: slst, 1 sc, 57 hdc, change to Vanilla, slst into next st of Round 5.
Strands 4–6 (3 strands): repeat strands 1–3.
Strand 7: ch16, and starting in third ch from hook: 14 hdc, change to Opaline Glass, slst into next st of Round 5.
Strand 8: ch16, and starting in third ch from hook: 14 hdc, change to Salmon, slst into next st of Round 5.
Strand 9: ch16, and starting in third ch from hook: 14 hdc, change to Vanilla, slst into next st of Round 5.
Strands 10–12 (3 strands): repeat strands 7–9.
Strands 13–15 (3 strands): repeat strands 1–3.
Strands 16–18 (3 strands): repeat strands 1–3.
Strands 19–21 (3 strands): repeat strands 1–3.
Strands 22–24 (3 strands): repeat strands 1–3.
Strands 25–27 (3 strands): repeat strands 1–3.
Strands 28–30 (3 strands): repeat strands 1–3.
Fasten off and weave in ends (23).

PART 2

Join Vanilla yarn into the first BLO of Round 3 of part 1 (24).
Strand 1: ch63, and starting in second ch from hook: slst, 1 sc, 60 hdc, change to Opaline Glass, slst into next BLO of Round 3.
Strand 2: ch63, and starting in second ch from hook: slst, 1 sc, 60 hdc, change to Salmon, slst into next BLO of Round 3.
Strand 3: ch19, and starting in third ch from hook: 17 hdc, change to Vanilla, slst into next BLO of Round 3.
Strand 4: ch19, and starting in third ch from hook: 17 hdc, change to Opaline Glass, slst into next BLO of Round 3.
Strand 5: ch19, and starting in third ch from hook: 17 hdc, change to Salmon, slst into next BLO of Round 3.
Strand 6: repeat strand 3.
Strands 7 and 8 (2 strands): repeat strands 1 and 2.
Strand 9: ch63, and starting in second ch from hook: slst, 1 sc, 60 hdc, change to Vanilla, 1 sc into next BLO of Round 3.
Strands 10–12 (3 strands): repeat strands 1, 2, and 9.
Strands 13–15 (3 strands): repeat strands 1, 2, and 9.
Strands 16–18 (3 strands): repeat strands 1, 2, and 9.
Fasten off and weave in ends (25).

23

24

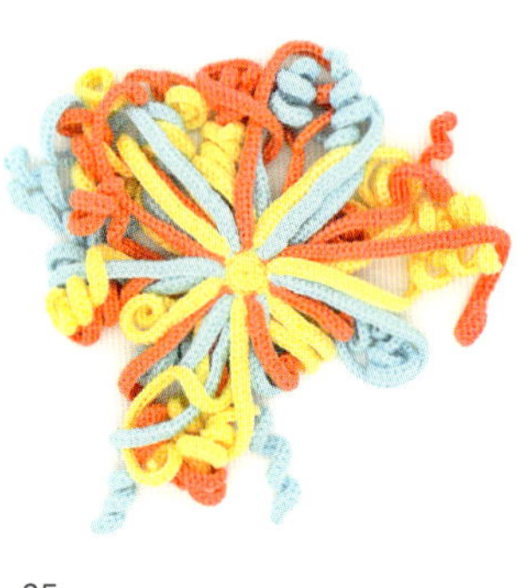
25

26

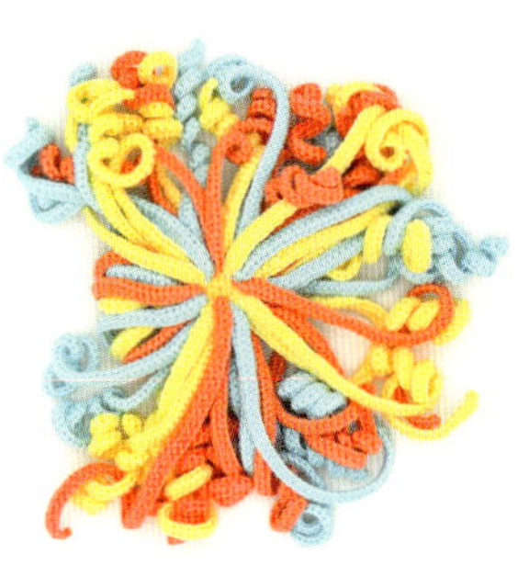
27

28

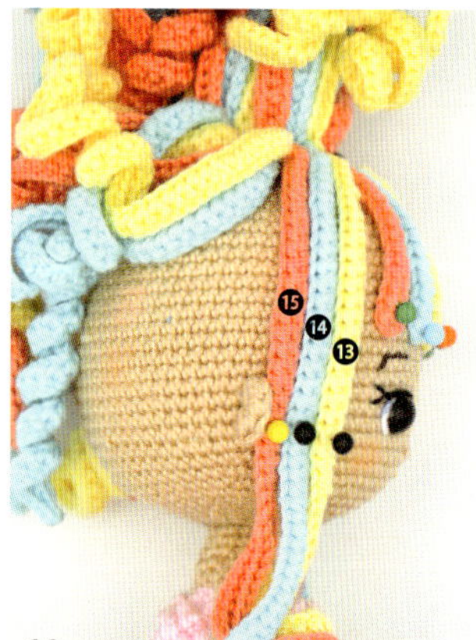

29

PART 3

Join Vanilla yarn into the first BLO of Round 2 of part 1 (26).
Strand 1: ch66, and starting in second ch from hook: slst, 1 sc, 63 hdc, change to Opaline Glass, slst into next BLO of Round 2.
Strand 2: ch22, and starting in third ch from hook: 20 hdc, change to Salmon, slst into next BLO of Round 2.
Strand 3: ch22, and starting in third ch from hook: 20 hdc, change to Vanilla, slst into next BLO of Round 2.
Strand 4: repeat strand 1.
Strand 5: ch66, and starting in second ch from hook: slst, 1 sc, 63 hdc, change to Salmon, slst into next BLO of Round 2.
Strand 6: ch66, and starting in second ch from hook: slst, 1 sc, 63 hdc, change to Vanilla, slst into next BLO of Round 2.
Strands 7–9 (3 strands): repeat strands 1, 5 and 6.
Strands 10–12 (3 strands): repeat strands 1, 5 and 6.
Fasten off and weave in ends (27).

ATTACH THE HAIR

Arrange the hair on the head, starting by placing the center of the MR of the hair on the center of the MR of the head. Hold in place with a pin.
Holding parts 2 and 3 together on top of the head with hair elastic will make things easier.
Part 1: position strands 4, 5, 6, 13, 14 and 15 on each side of the face (28, 29).
Position strands 7–12 on the forehead (30).
Place all the remaining strands around the head (31). It does not matter if there are a few little gaps between the strands – they will be filled in later.
Stick down the strands one by one, applying glue to each strand. Hold in place with pins until the glue has dried.
Part 2: position strands 3–6 on the forehead (32).
Position strands 1, 2, 7, and 8 in front of the ears (33, 34).
Distribute all the remaining strands over the strands of part 1, covering any little gaps (35).
Stick down the strands one by one.
Part 3: position strands 2 and 3 on the forehead (36).
Arrange all the remaining strands (37).
Stick down the strands one by one, only applying glue at the top.

Accessories

HORN

Note: work in spiral rounds.

Using Mustard, make MR.
Round 1: 4 sc into MR. (4 sts)
Round 2: inc in each st around. (8 sts)
Round 3: 1 sc BLO of each st around.
Round 4: [3 sc BLO, inc BLO] twice. (10 sts)
Round 5: 1 sc BLO of each st around.
Round 6: [4 sc BLO, inc BLO] twice. (12 sts)
Round 7: 1 sc BLO of each st around.
Round 8: [5 sc BLO, inc BLO] twice. (14 sts)
Round 9: 1 sc BLO of each st around.
Fasten off, leaving sufficient yarn for sewing to to the head (38).
Stuff.
Sew the horn to the center of the top of the fringe (39, 40).

UNICORN EARS (MAKE 2)

Note: work in spiral rounds.

Part 1

Using Mustard, make MR.
Round 1: 1 sc, 1 hdc, 1 dc, 2 tr, 1 dc, 1 hdc, 1 sc into MR. (8 sts)
Fasten off and weave in ends.

Part 2

Using Marble, make MR.
Round 1: 1 sc, 1 hdc, 1 dc, 2 tr, 1 dc, 1 hdc, 1 sc into MR. (8 sts)
Do not cut the yarn. Lay parts 1 and 2 on top of each other, WS together, aligning the sts.
Work the first inc of Round 2 into both the first st of Round 1 of Part 2 and the last st of Round 1 of Part 1 (41).
Round 2: inc, hdc-inc, dc-inc, tr-inc, ch1, tr-inc, dc-inc, hdc-inc, inc. (16 sts)
Fasten off, leaving sufficient yarn for sewing to the head (42).
Sew one ear on each side of the horn (43).

FLOWER

Note: work the flower along a foundation chain.

Using Peony Pink, ch12, and start in third ch from hook.
Row 1: [3 dc into same st, ch1, 1 sc, 3 hdc into next st, ch1, 1 sc] twice, 3 dc into next st, ch1, 1 sc.
Fasten off, leaving sufficient yarn for sewing to the head.
Roll the chain up on itself to get 1 flower and hold in place with 1 st in the center, taking the needle through all the thicknesses (44).
Sew the flower to the head between the horn and one ear (45).

38 39 40 41 42 43 44 45

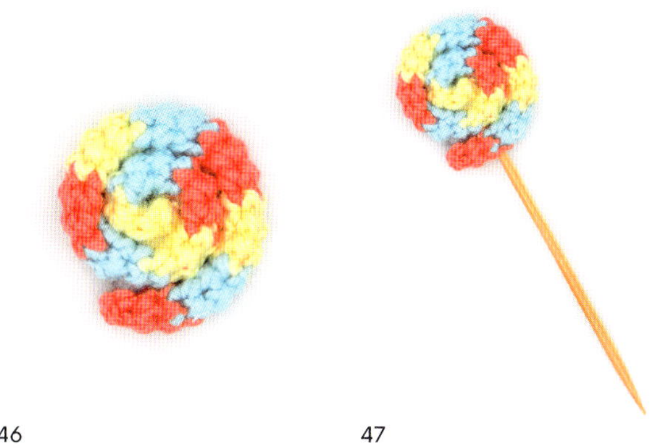

46 47

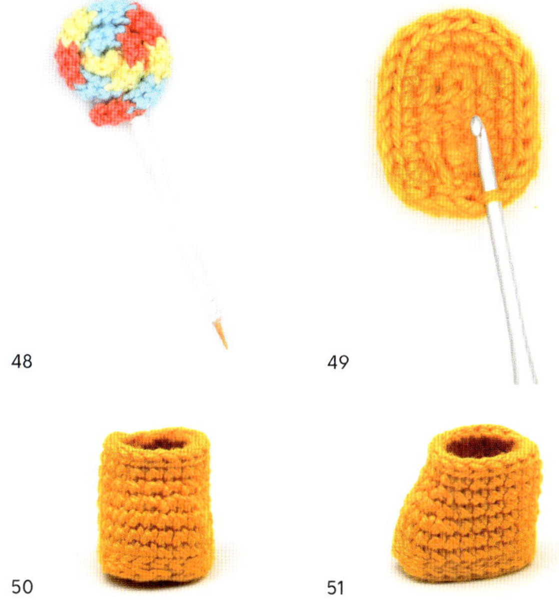

48 49 50 51

LOLLIPOP

Note: do not stuff. Work in spiral rounds.

Using Vanilla, make MR.
Round 1: 5 sc into MR. (5 sts)
Rounds 2 and 3 (2 rounds): 1 sc in each st around.
Change to Opaline Glass.
Rounds 4–6 (3 rounds): 1 sc in each st around.
Change to Salmon.
Rounds 7–9 (3 rounds): 1 sc in each st around.
Change to Vanilla.
Rounds 10–12 (3 rounds): 1 sc in each st around.
Change to Opaline Glass.
Rounds 13–15 (3 rounds): 1 sc in each st around.
Change to Salmon.
Rounds 16–18 (3 rounds): 1 sc in each st around.
Change to Vanilla.
Rounds 19–21 (3 rounds): 1 sc in each st around.
Change to Opaline Glass.
Rounds 22–24 (3 rounds): 1 sc in each st around.
Change to Salmon.
Rounds 25–27 (3 rounds): 1 sc in each st around.
Change to Vanilla.
Rounds 28–30 (3 rounds): 1 sc in each st around.
Change to Opaline Glass.
Rounds 31–33 (3 rounds): 1 sc in each st around.
Change to Salmon.
Rounds 34–36 (3 rounds): 1 sc in each st around.
Cut the yarn and fasten off.
Apply glue along the full length of the piece and roll up (46).
Hold in place using a pin until the glue has dried.
Apply some glue to one end of a toothpick and insert into the lollipop (47).
Wind the Marble yarn around the toothpick and stick into place, leaving the second stitch visible (48).

Shoes (make 2)

SOLES

Using Mustard, make the soles according to instructions in Standard Parts: Soles of the Shoes.

MAIN BODY OF SHOE

Join Mustard yarn to BLO of third slst of previous round (49).
Round 1: 25 sc BLO, slst to join. (25 sts)
Rounds 2 and 3 (2 rounds): ch1, 1 sc in each st around, slst to join.
Round 4: ch1, 7 sc [1 sc, dec] 4 times, 6 sc, slst to join. (21 sts)
Round 5: ch1, 8 sc, dec, 3 sc, dec, 6 sc, slst to join. (19 sts)
Round 6: ch1, 1 sc in each st around.
Round 7: slst in each st around.
Fasten off and weave in ends (50, 51).

The Little Companions

BIG COMPANION

Body

Using Opaline Glass, work the body according to instructions for the big body in Standard Parts: The Little Companions.

Horn

Note: work in spiral rounds.

Using Mustard, make MR.
Round 1: 4 sc into MR. (4 sts)
Round 2: [1 sc, inc] twice. (6 sts)
Round 3: [2 sc, inc] twice. (8 sts)
Round 4: [3 sc, inc] twice. (10 sts)
Round 5: [4 sc, inc] twice. (12 sts)
Round 6: [5 sc, inc] twice. (14 sts)
Fasten off, leaving sufficient yarn for sewing to body.
Stuff.
Sew the horn on top of the head, over the MR (52).

Ears (make 2)

Note: work in spiral rounds.

Using Opaline Glass, make MR.
Round 1: 4 sc into MR. (4 sts)
Round 2: [1 sc, inc] twice. (6 sts)
Round 3: [1 sc, inc] 3 times. (9 sts)
Round 4: 1 sc in each st around.
Fasten off, leaving sufficient yarn for sewing together.
Flatten the base of the ears and align the sts.
Sew together, taking the needle through both sides. Do not cut the yarn.
Using Marble, embroider 2 little marks in the center of the ear (53).
Sew one ear on each side of the horn (54).
Add some blush under the eyes (55).

MEDIUM-SIZED COMPANION

Body

Using Vanilla, work the body according to instructions for the medium-sized body in Standard Parts: The Little Companions.

Horn

Note: work in spiral rounds.

Using Mustard, make MR.
Round 1: 4 sc into MR. (4 sts)
Round 2: [1 sc, inc] twice. (6 sts)
Round 3: [2 sc, inc] twice. (8 sts)
Round 4: [3 sc, inc] twice. (10 sts)
Round 5: [4 sc, inc] twice. (12 sts)
Fasten off, leaving sufficient yarn for sewing to body.
Stuff.
Sew the horn on top of the head, over the MR.

Ears (make 2)

Note: work in spiral rounds.

Using Vanilla, make MR.
Round 1: 4 sc into MR. (4 sts)
Round 2: [1 sc, inc] twice. (6 sts)
Round 3: 1 sc in each st around.
Fasten off, leaving sufficient yarn for sewing together.
Flatten the base of the ears and align the sts. Sew together, taking the needle through both sides. Do not cut the yarn.
Using Marble, embroider 2 little marks in the center of the ear.
Sew one ear to each side of the horn.
Add some blush under the eyes (56).

SMALL COMPANION

Body

Using Salmon, work the body according to instructions for the small body in Standard Parts: The Little Companions.

Horn

Note: work in spiral rounds.

Using Mustard, make MR.
Round 1: 4 sc into MR. (4 sts)
Round 2: [1 sc, inc] twice. (6 sts)
Round 3: [2 sc, inc] twice. (8 sts)
Round 4: [3 sc, inc] twice. (10 sts)
Fasten off, leaving sufficient yarn for sewing to body.
Stuff.
Sew the horn on top of the head, over the MR.

Ears (make 2)

Note: work in spiral rounds.

Using Salmon, make MR.
Round 1: 4 sc into MR. (4 sts)
Round 2: [1 sc, inc] twice. (6 sts)
Fasten off, leaving sufficient yarn for sewing together.
Flatten the base of the ears and align the sts.
Sew together, taking the needle through both sides. Do not cut the yarn.
Using Marble, embroider 2 little marks in the center of the ear.
Sew one ear to each side of the horn.
Add some blush under the eyes (57).

Candies (make 6)

Note: work the candies in ovals around a foundation chain. Make 2 candies each in Vanilla, Salmon, and Opaline Glass.

Ch31 and start in the second ch from hook.
Round 1: 29 sc, (3 sc) in next ch, 29 sc down other side of foundation ch. (61 sts)
Work an invisible finish.
Fasten off, leaving sufficient yarn for sewing together.
Sew into shape, passing the yarn through the center of the foundation chain every 3 sts and pulling on the yarn to draw tightly together (58, 59).
Tie a knot and weave in the end (60).

52
53
54
55
56
57
58
59
60

Tenshi

Tenshi travels the skies accompanied by her little companions and sprinkles a little magic across the world. She speaks to the stars and grants all wishes.

Finished Size

Tenshi: approx 8¼in (21cm) tall
Companions: between 1½in (4cm) and 2¼in (6cm) tall

Note :
Size may vary depending on your gauge (tension) and the yarn used

Tools and Materials

Yarn and Colors Must-Have yarn in the following colors:

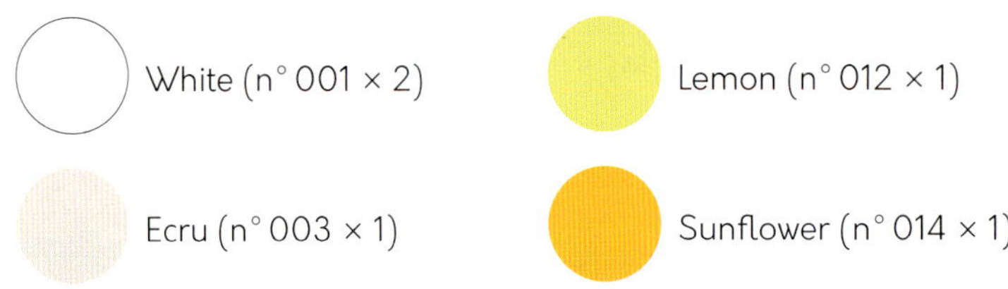

White (n° 001 × 2)
Lemon (n° 012 × 1)
Ecru (n° 003 × 1)
Sunflower (n° 014 × 1)

Yarn and Colors Glamour yarn in the following color:

Gold (n° 089 × 1)

US 4 (2.00mm) and US 4/0 (1.75mm) crochet hooks
Fiberfill stuffing
2 x 7mm safety eyes
Basic tool kit
(see Materials)

Instructions

Note: always use X-shaped stitches and joined rounds, unless stated otherwise.

Legs (make 2)

Using Ecru, make MR.
Round 1: 6 sc into MR, slst to join. (6 sts)
Round 2: ch1, inc in each st around, slst to join. (12 sts)
Round 3: ch1, [1 sc, inc] 6 times, slst to join. (18 sts)
Rounds 4 and 5 (2 rounds): ch1, 1 sc in each st around, slst to join.
Round 6: ch1, 6 sc, dec 3 times, 6 sc, slst to join. (15 sts)
Round 7: ch1, 5 sc, dec, 1 sc, dec, 5 sc, slst to join. (13 sts)
Rounds 8–12 (5 rounds): ch1, 1 sc in each st around, slst to join.
Round 13: ch1, 2 sc, inc, 7 sc, inc, 2 sc, slst to join. (15 sts)
Rounds 14–16 (3 rounds): ch1, 1 sc in each st around, slst to join.
Round 17: ch1, 2 sc, dec, 7 sc, dec, 2 sc, slst to join. (13 sts)
Round 18: ch1, 2 sc, inc, 7 sc, inc, 2 sc, slst to join. (15 sts)
Stuff the foot.
Round 19: ch1, 3 sc, inc, 7 sc, inc, 3 sc, slst to join. (17 sts)
Round 20: ch1, 1 sc in each st around, slst to join.
Round 21: ch1, 4 sc, inc, 7 sc, inc, 4 sc, slst to join. (19 sts)
Round 22: ch1, 1 sc in each st, slst to join.
Round 23: ch1, 5 sc, inc, 7 sc, inc, 5 sc, slst to join. (21 sts)
Round 24: ch1, 1 sc in each st around, slst to join.
Round 25: ch1, 1 sc in each st around, change to White, slst to join.

Round 26: ch1, 1 sc in each st around, slst to join.
Round 27: ch1, 1 sc in each st around, slst on RS to join. Mark last slst.
Leg 1: fasten off and weave in ends. Stuff leg firmly. Set aside.
Leg 2: repeat steps as for leg 1, but at end, work last slst on WS. Stuff leg firmly. Do not mark last slst, do not cut yarn, but continue as follows:

Body

Note: see Diagram I, Techniques: Joining the Legs.

Round 28: ch1, 6 sc into leg 2, ch2, [1 sc into fourth st before marked slst, 3 sc, 1 sc into same st as marked slst, 16 sc] on leg 1, 2 sc into ch2, 15 sc into remaining sts of leg 2, slst to join. (46 sts)
Round 29: ch1, 6 sc into leg 2, 2 sc in opposite side of ch2, then [dec, 21 sc] on leg 1, and [dec, 13 sc] on remaining sts of leg 2, slst to join. (44 sts)

Note: stuff as you go along.

Rounds 30–33 (4 rounds): ch1, 1 sc in each st around, slst to join.
Round 34: ch1, 1 sc in each st around, work an additional 7 sc in order to start next round in middle of back, slst to join.
Round 35: ch1, 15 sc, dec, 10 sc, dec, 15 sc, slst to join. (42 sts)
Round 36: ch1, 1 sc in each st around, slst to join.
Round 37: ch1, 14 sc, dec, 10 sc, dec, 14 sc, slst to join. (40 sts)
Round 38: ch1, 1 sc in each st around, slst BLO to join.
Round 39: ch1, [8 sc BLO, dec BLO] 4 times, slst to join. (36 sts)
Round 40: ch1, 1 sc in each st around, slst BLO to join. (36 sts)
Round 41: ch1, 1 sc BLO of each st around, slst to join.
Round 42: ch1, [7 sc, dec] 4 times, slst to join. (32 sts)
Round 43: ch1, 1 sc in each st around, slst to join.
Round 44: ch1, [6 sc, dec] 4 times, slst to join. (28 sts)
Round 45: ch1, 1 sc in each st around, slst to join.
Round 46: ch1, [5 sc, dec] 4 times, slst to join. (24 sts)
Round 47: ch1, 1 sc in each st around, slst to join.
Round 48: ch1, 6 sc, dec, 12 sc, dec, 2 sc, slst to join. (22 sts)
Round 49: ch1, 1 sc in each st around, slst to join.
Round 50: ch1, 6 sc, dec, 9 sc, dec, 3 sc, change to Lemon. (20 sts)
Round 51: slst BLO of each st around.
Round 52: ch1, 1 sc BLO of each st around, change to Ecru. (20 sts)
Round 53: slst BLO of each st around.
Round 54: ch1, 1 sc BLO of each st around, slst to join. (20 sts)
Round 55: ch1, [3 sc, dec] 4 times, slst to join. (16 sts)
Round 56: ch1, [3 sc, dec] twice, 4 sc, dec, slst to join. (13 sts)
Rounds 57–67 (11 rounds): ch1, 1 sc in each st around, slst to join.
Round 68: ch1, 5 sc, dec, 6 sc, slst to join. (12 sts)

Note: strengthen the neck (see Techniques: Strengthening the Neck).

Round 69: ch1, dec 6 times, slst to join. (6 sts)
Cut the yarn and fasten off *(1)*.

Skirt

PART 1

Holding the body neck down, join White yarn to FLO of st on back of body at Round 38 *(2)*.
Round 1: 40 sc FLO, slst to join. (40 sts)
Round 2: ch2, dc-inc 40 times, slst to join. (80 sts)
Round 3: ch2, dc-inc 80 times, slst to join. (160 sts)
Round 4: ch2, 1 dc in each st around, slst to join.
Round 5: ch2, [14 dc, 1 dc-dec] 10 times, slst to join. (150 sts)
Rounds 6 and 7 (2 rounds): ch2, 1 dc in each st around, slst to join.
Round 8: ch2, 1 dc in each st around, change to Lemon and Gold worked together, slst to join.
Round 9: ch2, 1 sc, [ch2, 1 sc] 149 times, slst to join.
Fasten off and weave in ends *(3)*.

PART 2

Holding the body neck down, join White yarn to FLO of st on back of body at Round 40 (4).
Round 1: 36 sc FLO, slst to join. (36 sts)
Round 2: ch2, dc-inc 36 times, slst to join. (72 sts)
Round 3: ch2, dc-inc 72 times, slst to join. (144 sts)
Round 4: ch2, 1 dc in each st around, slst to join.
Round 5: ch2, [14 dc, dc-dec] 9 times, slst to join. (135 sts)
Round 6: ch2, 1 dc in each st around, slst to join.
Round 7: ch2, 1 dc in each st around, change to White and Gold worked together, slst to join.
Round 8: ch2, 1 sc, [ch2, 1 sc] 134 times, slst to join.
Fasten off and weave in ends (5).
Using Gold, embroider some little stars on the bodice and a line around the neck (6).

Arms (make 2)

Using Ecru, make MR.
Round 1: 6 sc into MR, slst to join. (6 sts)
Round 2: ch1, [1 sc, inc] 3 times, slst to join. (9 sts)
Round 3: ch1, [2 sc, inc] 3 times, slst to join. (12 sts)
Round 4: ch1, 1 sc in each st around, slst to join.
Round 5: ch1, 5 sc, dec, 5 sc, slst to join. (11 sts)
Round 6: ch1, 5 sc, 1 3sc-bo (= thumb), 5 sc, slst to join.
Round 7: ch1, 5 sc, dec, 2 sc, dec, slst to join. (9 sts)
Round 8: ch1, 1 sc in each st around, slst to join.
Round 9: ch1, 5 sc, dec, 2 sc, slst to join. (8 sts)
Stuff hand firmly.
Rounds 10–18 (9 rounds): ch1, 1 sc in each st around, slst to join.
Round 19: ch1, 4 sc, dec, 2 sc, slst to join. (7 sts)
Rounds 20–23 (4 rounds): ch1, 1 sc in each st around, slst to join.
Round 24: ch1, 1 sc in each st around, slst on RS to join.
Stuff the arms lightly halfway.

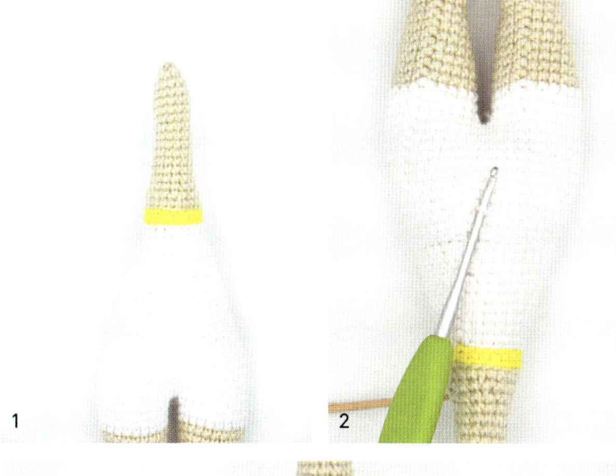
1 2

3

4

5 6

Flatten out the opening then work 3 sc through both thicknesses at the same time to close.
Fasten off, leaving sufficient yarn for sewing to body *(7)*.
Sew one arm to each side of the body between Rounds 54 and 55, ensuring that the thumbs are positioned at the front *(8, 9)*.

7

8

9

Wings (make 2)

PART 1 (MAKE 2)

Using White and Gold together, make MR.
Round 1: 6 sc into MR. (6 sts)
Round 2: inc in each st around. (12 sts)
Rounds 3–10 (8 rounds): 1 sc in each st around.
Cut the yarn and work an invisible finish.

PART 2 (MAKE 2)

Using White and Gold together, make MR.
Round 1: 6 sc into MR. (6 sts)
Round 2: inc in each st around. (12 sts)
Rounds 3–9 (7 rounds): 1 sc in each st around.
Cut the yarn and work an invisible finish.

PART 3 (MAKE 2)

Using White and Gold together, make MR.
Round 1: 6 sc into MR. (6 sts)
Round 2: inc in each st around. (12 sts)
Rounds 3–8 (6 rounds): 1 sc in each st around.
On next round, bring the 3 parts together as follows:

Round 9: 2 sc, 6 sc into Part 2, 12 sc into Part 1, 6 sc in remaining sts of Part 2, 10 sc in remaining sts of Part 3. (36 sts)
Round 10: 1 sc in each st around.
Round 11: [4 sc, dec] 6 times. (30 sts)
Round 12: [3 sc, dec] 6 times. (24 sts)
Round 13: [2 sc, dec] 6 times. (18 sts)
Round 14: [1 sc, dec] 6 times. (12 sts)
Round 15: dec 6 times. (6 sts)
Fasten off, leaving sufficient yarn for sewing to the body *(10)*.
Sew the wings to the back *(11)*.

10

11

Head

Using Ecru, make MR.
Round 1: 6 sc into MR, slst to join. (6 sts)
Round 2: ch1, inc in each st around, slst to join. (12 sts)
Round 3: ch1, [1 sc, inc] 6 times, slst to join. (18 sts)
Round 4: ch1, [1 sc, inc, 1 sc] 6 times, slst to join. (24 sts)
Round 5: ch1, [3 sc, inc] 6 times, slst to join. (30 sts)
Round 6: ch1, [2 sc, inc, 2 sc] 6 times, slst to join. (36 sts)
Round 7: ch1, [5 sc, inc] 6 times, slst to join. (42 sts)
Round 8: ch1, [3 sc, inc, 3 sc] 6 times, slst to join. (48 sts)
Round 9: ch1, [7 sc, inc] 6 times, slst to join. (54 sts)
Round 10: ch1, [4 sc, inc, 4 sc] 6 times, slst to join. (60 sts)
Round 11: ch1, 1 sc in each st around, slst to join.
Round 12: ch1, [9 sc, inc] 6 times, slst to join. (66 sts)
Round 13: ch1, 1 sc in each st around, slst to join.
Round 14: ch1, 16 sc, inc, 32 sc, inc, 16 sc, slst to join. (68 sts)
Rounds 15–23 (9 rounds): ch1, 1 sc in each st around, slst to join.
Round 24: ch1, 28 sc, ch1, sk 1 st, 10 sc, ch1, sk 1 st, 28 sc, slst to join.
Round 25: ch1, 28 sc, 1 sc into ch, 10 sc, 1 sc into ch, 28 sc, slst to join.
Round 26: ch1, 16 sc, dec, 32 sc, dec, 16 sc, slst to join. (66 sts)
Round 27: ch1, 1 sc in each st around, slst to join.
Round 28: ch1, 15 sc, dec, 32 sc, dec, 15 sc, slst to join. (64 sts)
Insert the eyes into the holes formed by the skipped sts in Round 24.
Round 29: ch1, [14 sc, dec] 4 times, slst to join. (60 sts)
Round 30: ch1, [4 sc, dec, 4 sc] 6 times, slst to join. (54 sts)
Round 31: ch1, [7 sc, dec] 6 times, slst to join. (48 sts)
Round 32: ch1, [4 sc, dec] 8 times, slst to join. (40 sts)

Round 33: ch1, [3 sc, dec] 8 times, slst to join. (32 sts)
Start to stuff.
Round 34: ch1, [2 sc, dec] 8 times, slst to join. (24 sts)
Round 35: ch1, [1 sc, dec] 8 times, slst BLO to join. (16 sts)
Round 36: ch1, 1 sc BLO of each st around, slst to join.
Rounds 37–41 (5 rounds): ch1, 1 sc in each st around, slst to join.
Fasten off and weave in ends. Complete the stuffing.
Push Rounds 36–41 inside the head (12).
Using White floss, embroider the whites of the eyes (13), then add a touch of Blue floss to the sides of the eyes (14).
Using Black floss embroider the black above the eyes (15) and finish by embroidering the eyelashes (16).
Using Brown floss, embroider the eyebrows between Rounds 20 and 22 (17).
Using Ecru, embroider the nose between Rounds 26 and 27.
Use a brush and some blush to add a little color to the cheeks and above the nose (18).

Note: the circumference of the head once stuffed is approximately 7½in (19cm).

EARS (MAKE 2)

Using Ecru, make MR.
Round 1: 1 sc, 4 hdc, 1 sc into MR. (6 sts)
Fasten off, leaving sufficient yarn for sewing to head.
Sew one ear to each side of the head between Rounds 23 and 27, leaving a gap of 8 sts between ear and eye (19, 20).

ATTACH THE HEAD

Using Ecru, attach the head according to instructions in Techniques: Attaching the Head. Leave 5 rounds in Ecru visible.

Hair

PART 1

Using Sunflower, make MR.
Round 1: 6 sc into MR, slst to join. (6 sts)
Round 2: ch1, inc in each st around, slst FLO to join. (12 sts)
Round 3: ch1, [1 sc FLO, inc FLO] 6 times, slst FLO to join. (18 sts)
Round 4: ch1, [1 sc FLO, inc FLO, 1 sc FLO] 6 times, slst to join. (24 sts)
Round 5: ch1, [3 sc, inc] 6 times, slst to join. (30 sts)
Do not cut the yarn. Continue with the strands of hair.

Note: it is the WS of the strands of hair that will be visible.

Note: if you are left-handed, reverse the order: start with strand 30 and finish with strand 1.

Strands 1–4 (4 strands): ch55, and starting in second ch from hook: slst, 1 sc, 52 hdc, slst into next st of Round 5 to join.
Strand 5: ch18, and starting in second ch from hook: slst, 16 sc, slst into next st of Round 5 to join.
Strand 6: ch55, and starting in second ch from hook: slst, 1 sc, 52 hdc, slst into next st of Round 5 to join.
Strand 7: ch9, and starting in second ch from hook: slst, 7 sc, slst into next st of Round 5 to join.
Strand 8: ch10, and starting in second ch from hook: slst, 8 sc, slst into next st of Round 5 to join.
Strand 9: ch11, and starting in second ch from hook: slst, 9 sc, slst into next st of Round 5 to join.
Strand 10: ch12, and starting in second ch from hook: slst, 10 sc, slst into next st of Round 5 to join.
Strand 11: ch13, and starting in second ch from hook: slst, 11 sc, slst into next st of Round 5 to join.

12

13

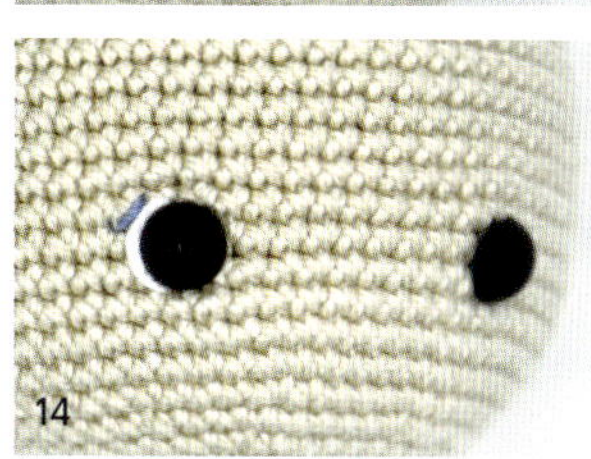
14

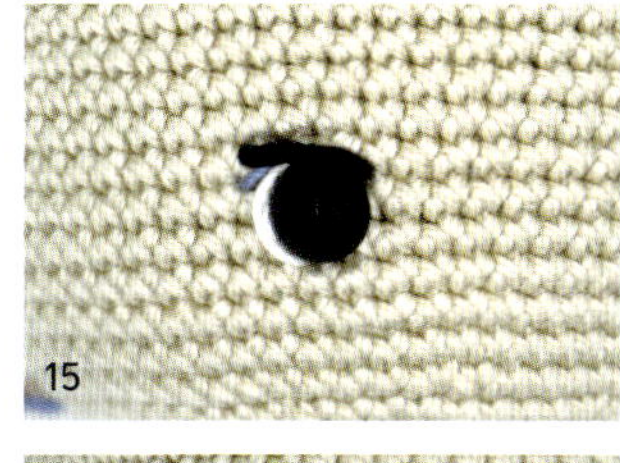
15

16

17

18

19

20

Strand 12: ch14, and starting in second ch from hook: slst, 12 sc, slst into next st of Round 5 to join.
Strand 13: ch15, and starting in second ch from hook: slst, 13 sc, slst into next st of Round 5 to join.
Strand 14: ch16, and starting in second ch from hook: slst, 14 sc, slst into next st of Round 5 to join.
Strand 15: ch17, and starting in second ch from hook: slst, 15 sc, slst into next st of Round 5 to join.
Strand 16: ch18, and starting in second ch from hook: slst, 16 sc, slst into next st of Round 5 to join.
Strands 17–30 (14 strands): ch55, and starting in second ch from hook: slst, 1 sc, 52 hdc, slst into next st of Round 5 to join.
Fasten off and weave in ends *(21)*.

PART 2

Note: if you are left-handed, reverse the order: start with strand 18 and finish with strand 1.

Join the Sunflower yarn to BLO of first st of Round 3 of Part 1 *(22)*.
Strands 1–18 (18 strands): ch58, and starting in second ch from hook: slst, 56 sc, slst BLO of next st of Round 5 to join.
Fasten off and weave in ends *(23)*.

PART 3

Note: if you are left-handed, reverse the order: start with strand 12 and finish with strand 1.

Join the Sunflower yarn to BLO of first st of Round 2 of Part 1 *(24)*.
Strands 1–12 (12 strands): ch61, and start in second ch from hook: slst, 59 sc, slst BLO of next st of Round 2 to join.
Fasten off and weave in ends *(25)*.

ATTACH THE HAIR

Arrange the hair on the head, starting by placing the center of the MR of the hair on the center of the MR of the head. Hold in place with a pin.
Holding Parts 2 and 3 together on top of the head with hair elastic will make things easier.
Part 1: position strands 1, 2, and 3 on the left side of the face *(26)*.
Leave strands 4, 5, and 6 for now.
Position strands 7–16 on the forehead *(27, 28)*.
Position strands 17–30 around the head *(29)*. It does not matter if there are a few little gaps between the strands – they will be filled in later.
Stick down the strands one by one, applying glue to each strand.
Hold in place with pins until the glue has dried.
Stick strand 4 to strands 1, 2 and 3 *(30)*.
Twist strand 6 and stick it down along strands 7–16 *(31)*.
Stick strand 5 to the forehead *(32)*.
Part 2: stick all the strands around the head, filling in any little gaps *(33–35)*.
Part 3: stick all the strands around the head *(36–38)*.

Accessories

HALO

Note: do not stuff. Work in spiral rounds.

Using Lemon and Gold together, make MR.

Round 1: 6 sc into MR. (6 sts)

Rounds 2–31 (30 rounds): 1 sc in each st around. (6 sts)

Fasten off, leaving sufficient yarn for sewing to hair.

Sew the two ends together to form a circle (39).

Sew or stick the back of the halo to the top of the head (40, 41).

31

32

33

34

35

36

37

38

39

40

41

MAGIC WAND

Note: work in spiral rounds.

Using Lemon and Gold together, make MR.
Round 1: 5 sc into MR. (5 sts)
Round 2: inc in each st around. (10 sts)
Round 3: [ch4, and starting in second ch from hook: slst, 1 sc, 1 hdc, sk 1 st of Round 2, slst into next st] 5 times.
Fasten off and weave in ends.
Make a second star, leaving sufficient yarn for sewing together (42).
Place the two stars one on top of the other, WS together.
Sew together using the tail of yarn from the second star.
Fasten off and weave in ends (43).
Wind the Gold yarn around a toothpick, gluing as you go, leaving the two ends free (44).
Apply some glue to one end of the toothpick and insert into the star (45).

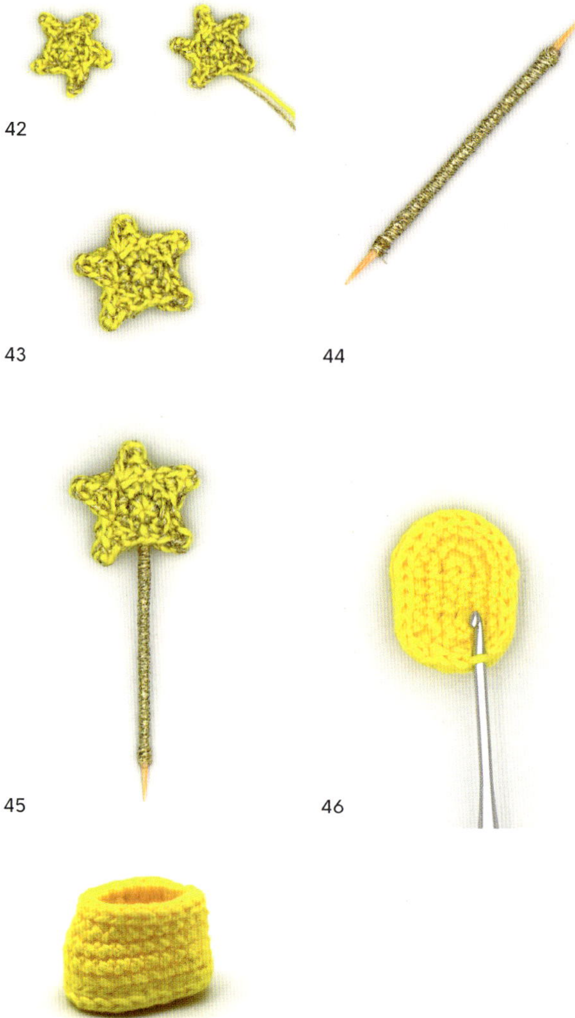

42

43

44

45

46

Shoes (make 2)

SOLES

Using Lemon, make the soles according to instructions in Standard Parts: Soles of the Shoes.

MAIN BODY OF SHOE

Join Lemon yarn to BLO of third slst of previous round (46).
Round 1: 25 sc BLO, slst to join. (25 sts)
Rounds 2 and 3 (2 rounds): ch1, 1 sc in each st around, slst to join.
Round 4: ch1, 7 sc [1 hdc, hdc-dec] 4 times, 1 hdc, 5 sc. (21 sts)
Round 5: slst in each st around.
Fasten off and weave in ends (47).
Using Gold, embroider in back stitch under the slsts of Round 5 (48).
For the laces, thread a strand of Lemon from one side of the leg to the other, between Rows 6 and 7 (49).
Continue threading it through in the same direction between Rows 11 and 12 (50) and Rows 15 and 16 (51).
Bring the strand back down, threading it back between Rows 11 and 12, then Rows 6 and 7 (52). With the other end of the yarn, repeat these steps to form the same pattern on the back of the leg (53).
Fasten off and weave in ends.
Repeat on leg 2.

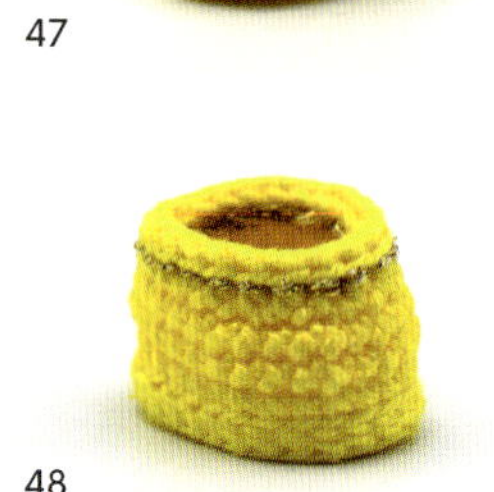

47

48

49 50

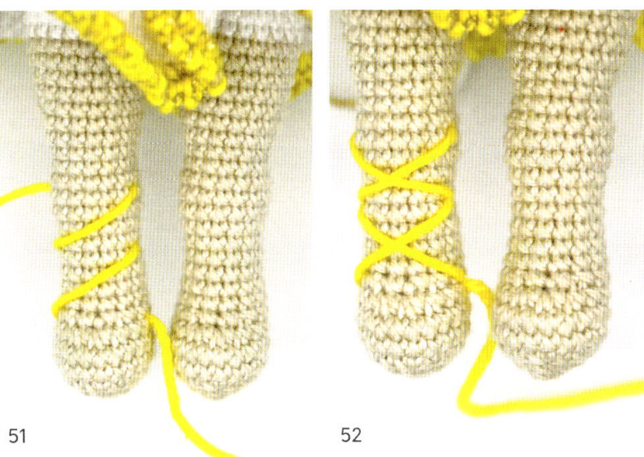
51 52

53

The Little Companions

BIG COMPANION

Body

Using White, work the body according to instructions for the big body in Standard Parts: The Little Companions.

Halo

Note: work the halo along a foundation chain.

Using a US 4/0 (1.75mm) hook and Gold, ch29 and start in second ch from hook.

Row 1: 28 sc. (28 sts)

Fasten off, leaving sufficient yarn for sewing to body.

Sew the two ends together to form a circle (54).

Note: it is the WS of the foundation chain that will be visible.

Sew the back of the halo to the top of the head (55).

54

55

Wings (make 2)

Note: do not stuff. Work in spiral rounds.

Using White and Gold together, make MR.
Round 1: 6 sc into MR. (6 sts)
Round 2: inc in each st around. (12 sts)
Round 3: 1 sc in each st around.
Flatten the top of the wing and align the sts.
Work 6 sc into the stitches on both sides.
Ch1, turn, (1 3hdc-bo, 1 sc) 3 times.
Fasten off, leaving sufficient yarn for sewing to the body.
Bring the yarn out through the center of the MR *(56)*.
Sew the wings to each side of the body between Rounds 12 and 13 *(57)*.
Add some blush under the eyes *(58)*.

56

MEDIUM-SIZED COMPANION

Body

Using White, work the body according to instructions for the medium-sized body in Standard Parts: The Little Companions.

57

Halo

Note: the halo is worked along a foundation chain.

Using a US 4/0 (1.75mm) hook and Gold, ch25 and start in second ch from hook.
Row 1: 24 sc. (24 sts)
Fasten off, leaving sufficient yarn for sewing to the body.
Sew the two ends of the chain together to form a circle.

Note: it is the WS of the foundation chain that will be visible.

Sew the back of the halo to the top of the body.

58

Wings (make 2)

Note: do not stuff. Work in spiral rounds.

Using White and Gold together, make MR.
Round 1: 5 sc into MR. (5 sts)
Round 2: inc in each st around. (10 sts)
Round 3: 1 sc in each st around.
Flatten the top of the wing and align the sts.
Work 5 sc into the stitches on both sides.
Ch1, turn, (2hdc-bo, 1 sc) twice, 2hdc-bo.
Fasten off, leaving sufficient yarn for sewing to the body.
Bring the yarn out through the center of the MR.
Sew the wings to each side of the body between Rounds 9 and 10.
Add some blush under the eyes *(59)*.

59

SMALL COMPANION

Body

Using White, work the body according to instructions for the small body in Standard Parts: The Little Companions.

Halo

Note: work the halo along a foundation chain.

Using a US 4/0 (1.75mm) hook and Gold, ch21 and start in second ch from hook.
Row 1: 20 sc. (20 sts)
Fasten off, leaving sufficient yarn for sewing to body.
Sew the two ends of the chain together to form a circle.

Note: it is the WS of the foundation chain that will be visible.

Sew the back of the halo to the top of the body.

Wings (make 2)

Note: do not stuff. Work in spiral rounds.

Using White and Gold together, make MR.
Round 1: 6 sc into MR. (6 sts)
Round 2: [1 sc, inc] 3 times. (9 sts)
Round 3: 1 sc in each st around.
Flatten the top of the wing and align the sts.
Work 4 sc into the stitches on both sides.
For the right wing: ch1, turn, 1 3sc-bo, 1 sc, 1 2sc-bo, 1 sc.
For the left wing: ch1, turn, 1 sc, 1 2sc-bo, 1 sc, 1 3sc-bo.
Fasten off, leaving sufficient yarn for sewing to the body.
Bring the yarn out through the center of the MR.
Sew the wings to each side of the body between Rounds 8 and 9.
Add some blush under the eyes *(60)*.

60

Koneko

Koneko loves beautiful snowy landscapes and sleeping snuggled up to her little companions. It must be said that snowball fights are tiring!

Finished Size

Koneko: approx 8¼in (21cm) tall
Companions: between 1½in (4.5cm) and 2¼in (6cm) tall

Note :
Size may vary depending on your gauge (tension) and the yarn used

Tools and Materials

Yarn and Colors Must-Have yarn in the following colors:

Yarn and Colors Glamour yarn in the following color:

Silver (n° 094 × 1)

Yarn and Colors Furry yarn in the following colors:

White (n° 001 × 1)
Soft Grey (n° 095 × 1)

US 4 (2.00mm) and US F-5 (3.75mm) crochet hooks
Fiberfill stuffing
2 x 7mm safety eyes
Basic tool kit
(see Materials)

Instructions

Note: always use X-shaped stitches and joined rounds, unless stated otherwise.

Legs (make 2)

Using Must-Have Soft Grey, make MR.
Round 1: 6 sc into MR, slst to join. (6 sts)
Round 2: ch1, inc in each st around, slst to join. (12 sts)
Round 3: ch1, [1 sc, inc] 6 times, slst to join. (18 sts)
Rounds 4 and 5 (2 rounds): ch1, 1 sc in each st around, slst to join.
Round 6: ch1, 6 sc, dec 3 times, 6 sc, slst to join. (15 sts)
Round 7: ch1, 5 sc, dec, 1 sc, dec, 5 sc, slst to join. (13 sts)
Rounds 8 and 9 (2 rounds): ch1, 1 sc in each st around, slst to join.
Round 10: ch1, 1 sc in each st around, change to Shark Grey, slst to join.
Rounds 11 and 12 (2 rounds): ch1, 1 sc in each st, slst to join.
Round 13: ch1, 2 sc, inc, 7 sc, inc, 2 sc, slst to join. (15 sts)
Rounds 14–16 (3 rounds): ch1, 1 sc in each st around, slst to join.
Round 17: ch1, 2 sc, dec, 7 sc, dec, 2 sc, slst to join. (13 sts)
Round 18: ch1, 2 sc, inc, 7 sc, inc, 2 sc, slst to join. (15 sts)
Stuff the foot.
Round 19: ch1, 3 sc, inc, 7 sc, inc, 3 sc, slst to join. (17 sts)
Round 20: ch1, 1 sc in each st around, slst to join.
Round 21: ch1, 4 sc, inc, 7 sc, inc, 4 sc, slst to join. (19 sts)

Round 22: ch1, 1 sc in each st around, slst to join.
Round 23: ch1, 5 sc, inc, 7 sc, inc, 5 sc, slst to join. (21 sts)
Rounds 24–26 (3 rounds): ch1, 1 sc in each st around, slst to join.
Round 27: ch1, 1 sc in each st around, slst on RS to join. Mark last slst.
Leg 1: fasten off and weave in ends.
Stuff leg firmly. Set aside.
Leg 2: repeat steps as for leg 1, but at end, work last slst on WS to join.
Stuff leg firmly. Do not mark last slst, do not cut yarn, but continue as follows:

Body

Note: see Diagram 1, Techniques: Joining the Legs.

Round 28: ch1, 6 sc into leg 2, ch2, [1 sc into fourth st before marked slst, 3 sc, 1 sc into same st as marked slst, 16 sc] on leg 1, 2 sc into ch2, 15 sc into remaining sts of leg 2, slst to join. (46 sts)
Round 29: ch1, 6 sc into leg 2, 2 sc in opposite side of ch2, then dec, 21 sc] on leg 1, [dec, 13 sc] on remaining sts of leg 2, slst to join. (44 sts)

Note: stuff as you go along.

Rounds 30–33 (4 rounds): ch1, 1 sc in each st around, slst to join.
Round 34: ch1, 1 sc in each st around, work an additional 7 sc in order to start next round in middle of back, slst to join.
Round 35: ch1, 15 sc, dec, 10 sc, dec, 15 sc, slst to join. (42 sts)
Round 36: ch1, 1 sc in each st around, slst to join.
Round 37: ch1, 14 sc, dec, 10 sc, dec, 14 sc, slst to join. (40 sts)
Round 38: ch1, 1 sc in each st around, slst to join.
Round 39: ch1, [8 sc, dec] 4 times, slst to join. (36 sts)
Start to stuff.
Rounds 40 and 41 (2 rounds): ch1, 1 sc in each st around, slst to join.
Round 42: ch1, [7 sc, dec] 4 times, slst to join. (32 sts)
Round 43: ch1, 1 sc in each st around, slst to join.
Round 44: ch1, [6 sc, dec] 4 times, slst to join. (28 sts)
Round 45: ch1, 1 sc in each st around, slst to join.
Round 46: ch1, [5 sc, dec] 4 times, slst to join. (24 sts)
Round 47: ch1, 1 sc in each st around, slst to join.
Round 48: ch1, 6 sc, dec, 12 sc, dec, 2 sc, slst to join. (22 sts)
Round 49: ch1, 1 sc in each st around, slst to join.
Round 50: ch1, 6 sc, dec, 9 sc, dec, 3 sc, slst to join. (20 sts)
Round 51: ch1, [3 sc, dec] 4 times, slst to join. (16 sts)
Round 52: ch1, [3 sc, dec] twice, 4 sc, dec, change to Limestone. (13 sts)
Round 53: slst BLO of each st around.
Round 54: ch1, 1 sc BLO of each st around, slst to join.
Rounds 55–65 (11 rounds): ch1, 1 sc in each st around, slst to join.
Round 66: ch1, 5 sc, dec, 6 sc, slst to join. (12 sts)

Note: strengthen the neck (see Techniques: Strengthening the Neck)

Round 67: ch1, dec 6 times, slst to join. (6 sts)
Cut the yarn and fasten off (1).
Thread the Furry Soft Grey yarn twice around the bottom of the body between Rounds 32 and 34, then up and down the center front of the body (2).
Fasten off and weave in ends.

Arms (make 2)

Using Limestone, make MR.
Round 1: 6 sc into MR, slst to join. (6 sts)
Round 2: ch1, [1 sc, inc] 3 times, slst to join. (9 sts)
Round 3: ch1, [2 sc, inc] 3 times, slst to join. (12 sts)
Round 4: ch1, 1 sc in each st around, slst to join.
Round 5: ch1, 5 sc, dec, 5 sc, slst to join. (11 sts)
Round 6: ch1, 5 sc, 1 3sc-bo (= thumb), 5 sc, slst to join.
Round 7: ch1, 5 sc, dec, 2 sc, dec, slst to join. (9 sts)
Round 8: ch1, 1 sc in each st around, change to Shark Grey, slst to join.
Round 9: ch1, 5 sc, dec, 2 sc, slst to join. (8 sts)

Stuff hand firmly.
Rounds 10–18 (9 rounds): ch1, 1 sc in each st around, slst to join.
Round 19: ch1, 4 sc, dec, 2 sc, slst to join. (7 sts)
Rounds 20–23 (4 rounds): ch1, 1 sc in each st around, slst to join.
Round 24: ch1, 1 sc in each st around, slst on RS to join.
Stuff the arms lightly halfway.
Flatten out the opening then work 3 sc through both thicknesses at the same time to close.
Fasten off and cut, leaving enough yarn for sewing to body.

Thread the Furry Soft Grey yarn twice around the wrist (3).
Sew one arm to each side of the body at the last grey round, ensuring that the thumbs are positioned at the front (4).

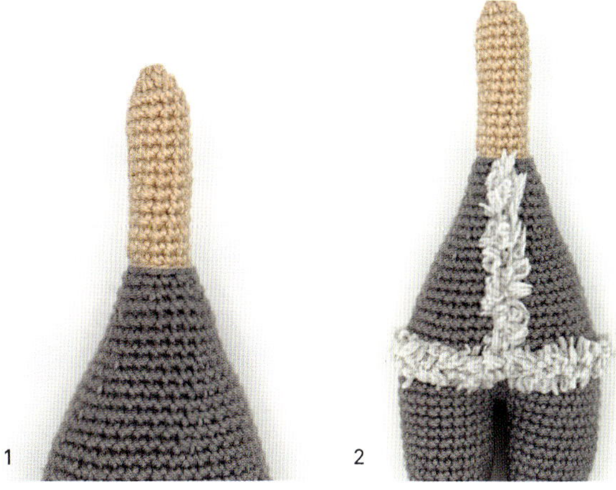
1 2

3

4

Head

Using Limestone, make MR
Round 1: 6 sc into MR, slst to join. (6 sts)
Round 2: ch1, inc in each st around, slst to join. (12 sts)
Round 3: ch1, [1 sc, inc] 6 times, slst to join. (18 sts)
Round 4: ch1, [1 sc, inc, 1 sc] 6 times, slst to join. (24 sts)
Round 5: ch1, [3 sc, inc] 6 times, slst to join. (30 sts)
Round 6: ch1, [2 sc, inc, 2 sc] 6 times, slst to join. (36 sts)
Round 7: ch1, [5 sc, inc] 6 times, slst to join. (42 sts)
Round 8: ch1, [3 sc, inc, 3 sc] 6 times, slst to join. (48 sts)
Round 9: ch1, [7 sc, inc] 6 times, slst to join. (54 sts)
Round 10: ch1, [4 sc, inc, 4 sc] 6 times, slst to join. (60 sts)
Round 11: ch1, 1 sc in each st around, slst to join.
Round 12: ch1, [9 sc, inc] 6 times, slst to join. (66 sts)
Round 13: ch1, 1 sc in each st around, slst to join.
Round 14: ch1, 16 sc, inc, 32 sc, inc, 16 sc, slst to join. (68 sts)
Rounds 15–23 (9 rounds): ch1, 1 sc in each st around, slst to join.
Round 24: ch1, 28 sc, ch1, sk 1 st, 10 sc, ch1, sk 1 st, 28 sc, slst to join.
Round 25: ch1, 28 sc, 1 sc into ch, 10 sc, 1 sc into ch, 28 sc, slst to join.
Round 26: ch1, 16 sc, dec, 32 sc, dec, 16 sc, slst to join. (66 sts)
Round 27: ch1, 1 sc in each st around, slst to join.
Round 28: ch1, 15 sc, dec, 32 sc, dec, 15 sc, slst to join. (64 sts)
Insert the eyes into the holes formed by the skipped sts in Round 24.
Round 29: ch1, [14 sc, dec] 4 times, slst to join. (60 sts)
Round 30: ch1, [4 sc, dec, 4 sc] 6 times, slst to join. (54 sts)
Round 31: ch1, [7 sc, dec] 6 times, slst to join. (48 sts)
Round 32: ch1, [4 sc, dec] 8 times, slst to join. (40 sts)
Round 33: ch1, [3 sc, dec] 8 times, slst to join. (32 sts)
Start to stuff.
Round 34: ch1, [2 sc, dec] 8 times, slst to join. (24 sts)
Round 35: ch1, [1 sc, dec] 8 times, slst BLO to join. (16 sts)
Round 36: ch1, 1 sc BLO of each st around, slst to join.
Rounds 37–41 (5 rounds): ch1, 1 sc in each st around, slst to join.
Fasten off and weave in ends. Complete the stuffing.

Push Rounds 36–41 inside the head (5).
Embroider the white of the eyes (6), then add a touch of blue to the sides of the eyes (7).
Embroider the black above the eyes (8).
Finish by embroidering the eyelashes (9).
Using the Black floss, embroider the eyebrows between Rounds 20 and 22 (10).
Using Limestone, embroider the nose between Rounds 26 and 27 (11).
Use a brush and some blush to add a little color to the cheeks and above the nose (12).

Note: the circumference of the head once stuffed is approximately 7½in (19cm).

5

6

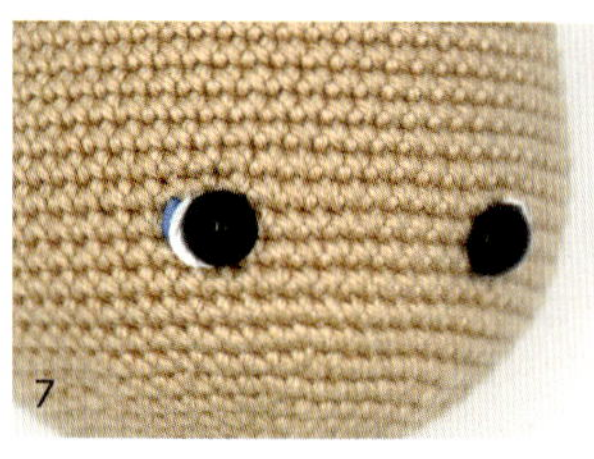
7

8

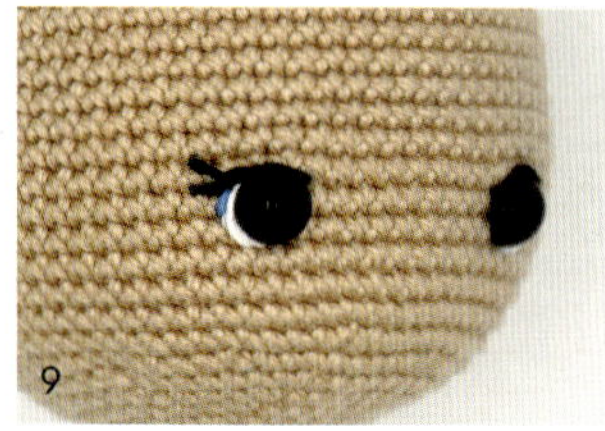
9

10

ATTACH THE HEAD

Using Limestone, attach the head according to instructions in Techniques: Attaching the Head. Leave 3 rounds in Limestone visible.

The Hood and the Hair

HOOD

Using Shark Grey, make MR.
Round 1: 6 sc into MR, slst to join. (6 sts)
Round 2: ch1, inc in each st around, slst to join. (12 sts)
Round 3: ch1, [1 sc, inc] 6 times, slst to join. (18 sts)
Round 4: ch1, [1 sc, inc, 1 sc] 6 times, slst to join. (24 sts)
Round 5: ch1, [3 sc, inc] 6 times, slst to join. (30 sts)
Round 6: ch1, [2 sc, inc, 2 sc] 6 times, slst to join. (36 sts)
Round 7: ch1, [5 sc, inc] 6 times, slst to join. (42 sts)
Round 8: ch1, [3 sc, inc, 3 sc] 6 times, slst to join. (48 sts)
Round 9: ch1, [7 sc, inc] 6 times, slst to join. (54 sts)
Round 10: ch1, [4 sc, inc, 4 sc] 6 times, slst to join. (60 sts)
Round 11: ch1, 1 sc in each st around, slst to join.
Round 12: ch1, [9 sc, inc] 6 times, slst to join. (66 sts)
Round 13: ch1, 16 sc, inc, 32 sc, inc, 16 sc, slst to join. (68 sts)
Round 14: ch1, [16 sc, inc] 4 times, slst to join. (72 sts)
Rounds 15–23 (9 rounds): ch1, 1 sc in each st around, slst to join.
Fasten off and weave in ends.

11

12

13

HAIR

Part 1 (Fringe)

Note : it is the WS of the strands of hair that will be visible.

Join Black yarn to BLO of the fifty-first sc of Round 23 of the Hood (13).

Strand 1: ch7, and starting in third ch from hook: 5 hdc, sk 1 st, slst BLO of next st of Round 23 of Hood to join.

Strand 2: ch8, and starting in third ch from hook: 6 hdc, sk 1 st, slst BLO of next st of Round 23 of Hood to join.

Strand 3: ch9, and starting in third ch from hook: 7 hdc, sk 1 st, slst BLO of next st of Round 23 of Hood to join.

Strand 4: ch10, and starting in third ch from hook: 8 hdc, sk 1 st, slst BLO of next st of Round 23 of Hood to join.

Strands 5–8 (4 strands): ch11, and starting in third ch from hook: 9 hdc, sk 1 st, slst BLO of next st of Round 23 of Hood to join.

Strand 9: ch10, and starting in third ch from hook: 8 hdc, sk 1 st, slst BLO of next st of Round 23 of Hood to join.

Strand 10: ch9, and starting in third ch from hook: 7 hdc, sk 1 st, slst BLO of next st of Round 23 of Hood to join.

Strand 11: ch8, and starting in third ch from hook: 6 hdc, sk 1 st, slst BLO of next st of Round 23 of Hood to join.

Strand 12: ch7, and starting in third ch from hook: 5 hdc, sk 1 st, slst BLO of next st of Round 23 of Hood to join.

Fasten off and weave in ends.

Assembly

Place the hood on the head and stick the strands of Hair to the forehead (14, 15).

Part 2 (Braids)

Cut 12 strands of Black yarn, approximately 20in (51cm) long. Count 3 sts to the left from the middle of the back of the hood, and thread 2 strands of yarn through the fourth st. Do the same in the fifth and sixth sts (16). Plait a braid approximately 3¼in (8cm) long using these strands and hold in place with a knot using Black yarn (17).

Do the same on the right-hand side (18).

HOOD BRIM

Stick several strands of Furry Soft Grey around the head until the fur is thick enough.

Cut a short strand of yarn and knot it around the neck (19).

14 15

16

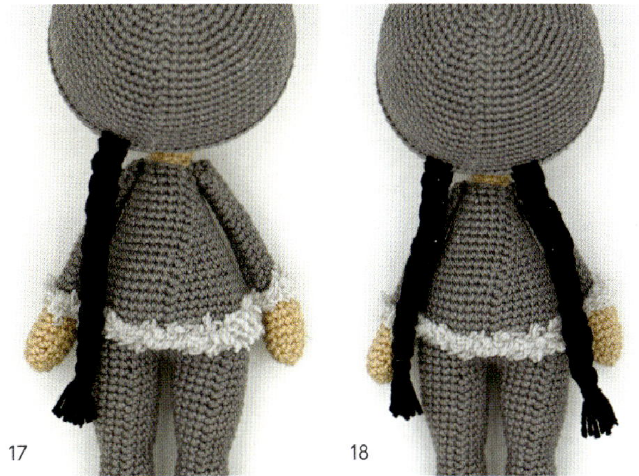

17 18

19

Ears (make 2)

Note: do not stuff. Work in spiral rounds.

Using Shark Grey and Silver together, make MR.
Round 1: 6 sc into MR. (6 sts)
Round 2: [1 sc, inc] 3 times. (9 sts)
Round 3: [2 sc, inc] 3 times. (12 sts)
Round 4: [3 sc, inc] 3 times. (15 sts)
Round 5: [4 sc, inc] 3 times. (18 sts)
Rounds 6–8 (3 rounds): 1 sc in each st around.
Flatten out the opening then work ch1, 9 sc through both thicknesses at the same time to close.
Fasten off and cut, leaving enough yarn for sewing to the Hood.
Using Must-Have Soft Grey, embroider the inside of the ear *(20)*.
Sew the ears to the hood *(21, 22)*.

20 21 22

Shoes (make 2)

SOLES

Using Shark Grey, make the soles according to instructions in Standard Parts: Soles of the Shoes.

MAIN BODY OF SHOE

Using Shark Grey and Silver together, join yarn to BLO of third slst of previous round *(23)*.
Round 1: 25 sc BLO, slst to join. (25 sts)
Rounds 2 and 3 (2 rounds): ch1, 1 sc in each st around, slst to join.
Round 4: ch1, 7 sc [1 sc, dec] 4 times, 6 sc, slst to join. (21 sts)
Round 5: ch1, 8 sc, dec, 3 sc, dec, 6 sc, slst to join. (19 sts)
Rounds 6–8 (3 rounds): ch1, 1 sc in each st around, slst to join.
Round 9: ch1, 1 sc in each st around, slst on RS to join.
Fasten off and weave in ends *(24)*.
Stick 2 strands of Furry Soft Grey around the tops of the shoes *(25)*.

23 24 25

Snowballs

Note: work in spiral rounds.

BIG SNOWBALL

Using Must-Have White, make MR.
Round 1: 6 sc into MR. (6 sts)
Round 2: inc in each st around. (12 sts)
Round 3: [1 sc, inc] 6 times. (18 sts)
Rounds 4 and 5 (2 rounds): 1 sc in each st around.
Round 6: [1 sc, dec] 6 times. (12 sts)
Stuff.
Round 7: dec 6 times. (6 sts)
Cut the yarn and fasten off.
Embroider all around the ball using Furry White *(26)*.

SMALL SNOWBALL

Using Must-Have White, make MR.
Round 1: 6 sc into MR. (6 sts)
Round 2: inc in each st around. (12 sts)
Rounds 3 and 4 (2 rounds): 1 sc in each st around.
Stuff.
Round 5: dec 6 times. (6 sts)
Cut the yarn and fasten off.
Embroider all around the ball using Furry White *(26)*.

The Little Companions

BIG COMPANION

Body

Using Shark Grey, work the body according to instructions for the big body in Standard Parts: The Little Companions.

Ears (make 2)

Using Shark Grey, make MR.
Round 1: 1 hdc, 2 sc, ch2, 2 sc, 1 hdc into MR. (8 sts)
Fasten off, leaving sufficient yarn for sewing to body.
Sew on the ears between Rounds 2 and 6 of the body *(27)*.

Tail

Using a US F-5 (3.75mm) hook and Furry Soft Grey, ch10.
Fasten off, leaving sufficient yarn for sewing to body.
Sew each end of the chain to the back, between Rounds 17 and 19 *(28)*.
Roll up the chain to form the tail *(29)*.
Add some blush under the eyes *(30)*.

MEDIUM-SIZED COMPANION

Body

Using Must-Have Soft Grey, work the body according to instructions for the medium-sized body in Standard Parts: The Little Companions.

Ears (make 2)

Using Must-Have Soft Grey, make MR.
Round 1: 1 hdc, 2 sc, ch2, 2 sc, 1 hdc into MR. (8 sts)
Fasten off, leaving sufficient yarn for sewing to the body.
Sew on the ears between Rounds 2 and 6 of the body.

Tail

Using a US F-5 (3.75mm) hook and Furry White, ch8.
Fasten off, leaving sufficient yarn for sewing to the body.
Sew each end of the chain to the back, between Rounds 14 and 16. Roll up the chain to form the tail.
Add some blush under the eyes *(31)*.

SMALL COMPANION

Body

Using Shark Grey, work the body according to instructions for the small body in Standard Parts: The Little Companions.

Ears (make 2)

Using Shark Grey, make MR.
Round 1: 2 sc, ch2, 2 sc into MR. (6 sts)
Fasten off, leaving sufficient yarn for sewing to body.
Sew on the ears between Rounds 2 and 6 of the body.

26 27 28 29 30 31 32

Tail

Using a US F-5 (3.75mm) hook and Furry Soft Grey, ch6.
Fasten off, leaving sufficient yarn for sewing to body.
Sew each end of the chain to the back, between Rounds 11 and 13. Roll up the chain to form the tail.
Add some blush under the eyes *(32)*.

Difficulty: ● ● ○

Mimi and her little companions love playing hide-and-seek in their cozy forest. But what they love the most is cuddles.

Finished Size

Mimi: approx 9½in (24cm) tall
Companions: between 2¼in (6cm) and 3in (7.5cm) tall

Note:

Size may vary depending on your gauge (tension) and the yarn used

Tools and Materials

Yarn and Colors Must-Have yarn in the following colors:

Ecru (n° 003 × 1)
Peony Pink (n° 038 × 1)
Marble (n° 102 × 1)
Vanilla (n° 010 × 1)
Blossom (n° 045 × 1)

Yarn and Colors Furry yarn in the following color:

Pearl (n° 043 × 1).

US 4 (2.00mm) crochet hook
Fiberfill stuffing
2 x 7mm safety eyes
Basic tool kit
(see Materials)

Instructions

Note: always use X-shaped stitches and joined rounds, unless stated otherwise.

Legs (make 2)

Using Marble, make MR.
Round 1: 6 sc into MR, slst to join. (6 sts)
Round 2: ch1, inc in each st around, slst to join. (12 sts)
Round 3: ch1, [1 sc, inc] 6 times, slst to join. (18 sts)
Rounds 4 and 5 (2 rounds): ch1, 1 sc in each st around, slst to join.
Round 6: ch1, 6 sc, dec 3 times, 6 sc, slst to join. (15 sts)
Round 7: ch1, 5 sc, dec, 1 sc, dec, 5 sc, slst to join. (13 sts)
Rounds 8–12 (5 rounds): ch1, 1 sc in each st around, slst to join.
Round 13: ch1, 2 sc, inc, 7 sc, inc, 2 sc, change to Ecru, slst BLO to join. (15 sts)
Round 14: ch1, 1 sc BLO of each st around, slst to join.
Rounds 15 and 16 (2 rounds): ch1, 1 sc in each st around, slst to join.
Round 17: ch1, 2 sc, dec, 7 sc, dec, 2 sc, slst to join. (13 sts)
Round 18: ch1, 2 sc, inc, 7 sc, inc, 2 sc, slst to join. (15 sts)
Stuff the foot.
Round 19: ch1, 3 sc, inc, 7 sc, inc, 3 sc, slst to join. (17 sts)
Round 20: ch1, 1 sc in each st around, slst to join.
Round 21: ch1, 4 sc, inc, 7 sc, inc, 4 sc, change to Blossom, slst BLO to join. (19 sts)
Round 22: ch1, inc BLO of each st around, slst to join. (38 sts)

Round 23: ch1, 1 sc in each st around, slst to join.
Round 24: ch1, [4 sc, dec] 6 times, 2 sc, slst to join. (32 sts)
Round 25: ch1, [3 sc, dec] 6 times, 2 sc, slst to join. (26 sts)
Round 26: ch1, [3 sc, dec] 5 times, 1 sc, slst to join. (21 sts)
Round 27: ch1, 1 sc in each st around, slst on RS to join.
Mark last slst.
Leg 1: fasten off and weave in ends.
Stuff leg firmly.
Holding the leg with the foot uppermost, join Marble yarn FLO of first st of Round 13 *(1)*, [ch2, slst] 15 times.
Fasten off and weave in ends *(2)*.
Join Marble FLO of first st of Round 21 in the same way as previously, [ch2, slst] 19 times.
Fasten off and weave in ends *(3)*.
Using Blossom, embroider little "V"s on the sock *(4)*.
Set aside.
Leg 2: repeat the steps as for leg 1, but work last slst on WS to join.
Stuff leg firmly. Do not mark last slst, do not cut yarn.

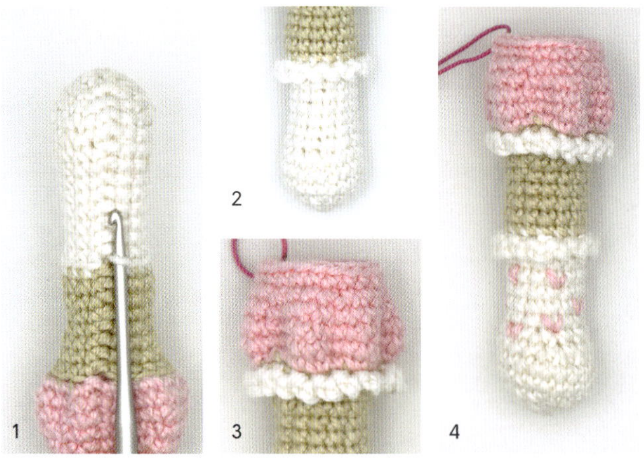

Body

Note: see Diagram 2, Techniques: Joining the Legs

Round 28: ch1, 8 sc into leg 2, ch2, [1 sc into fourth st before marked slst, 3 sc, 1 sc into same st as marked slst, 16 sc] on leg 1, 2 sc into ch2 and 13 sc into remaining sts of leg 2, slst to join. (46 sts)
Round 29: ch1, 8 sc into leg 2, 2 sc in opposite side of ch2, [dec, 21 sc] on leg 1, [dec, 11 sc] on remaining sts of leg 2, slst to join. (44 sts)

Note: stuff as you go along.

Rounds 30–33 (4 rounds): ch1, 1 sc in each st around, slst to join.
Round 34: ch1, 1 sc in each st around, work an additional 10 sc in order to start next round in middle of back, slst to join.
Round 35: ch1, 14 sc, dec, 11 sc, dec, 15 sc, slst to join. (42 sts)
Round 36: ch1, 1 sc in each st around, slst to join.
Round 37: ch1, 13 sc, dec, 11 sc, dec, 14 sc, slst to join. (40 sts)
Round 38: ch1, 1 sc in each st around, slst to join.
Round 39: ch1, [8 sc, dec] 4 times, slst to join. (36 sts)
Rounds 40 and 41 (2 rounds): ch1, 1 sc in each st around, slst to join.
Round 42: ch1, [7 sc, dec] 4 times, slst to join. (32 sts)
Round 43: ch1, 1 sc in each st around, slst to join.
Round 44: ch1, (6 sc, dec) 4 times, change to Marble, slst BLO to join. (28 sts)
Round 45: ch1, 1 sc BLO of each st around, slst to join.
Round 46: ch1, [5 sc, dec] 4 times, slst to join. (24 sts)
Round 47: ch1, 1 sc in each st around, slst to join.
Round 48: ch1, 6 sc, dec, 10 sc, dec, 4 sc, slst to join. (22 sts)
Round 49: ch1, 1 sc in each st around, slst to join.
Round 50: ch1, 5 sc, dec, 9 sc, dec, 4 sc, change to Ecru, slst BLO to join. (20 sts)
Round 51: ch1, [3 sc BLO, dec BLO] 4 times, slst to join. (16 sts)
Round 52: ch1, [3 sc, dec] twice, 4 sc, dec, slst to join. (13 sts)
Rounds 53–63 (11 rounds): ch1, 1 sc in each st around, slst to join.
Round 64: ch1, 5 sc, dec, 6 sc, slst to join. (12 sts)

Note: strengthen the neck (see Techniques: Strengthening the Neck).

Round 65: ch1, dec 6 times, slst to join. (6 sts)
Cut the yarn and fasten off *(5)*.
Holding the body neck down, join Peony Pink yarn to FLO of first st of Round 44 *(6)*, [(1 sc, 2 hdc, 1 sc) FLO of same st, slst] 14 times.
Fasten off and weave in ends.
Using Marble, embroider French knots in the 14 "wavelets" to hold them against the body *(7)*.
Holding the body neck down, join Blossom yarn to FLO of first st of Round 50 *(8)*, [ch2, slst] 20 times.
Fasten off and weave in ends *(9)*.
Using Blossom, embroider little "V"s on the top of the body *(10)*.

HEART

Using Peony Pink, make MR.
Round 1: ch3, 2 dc, 1 hdc, 1 sc, ch2, 1 sc, 1 hdc, 2 dc, ch3, slst into MR.
Fasten off and cut, leaving enough yarn for sewing to the body.
Sew the heart to center front of body *(11)*.

Arms (make 2)

Using Ecru, make MR.
Round 1: 6 sc into MR, slst to join. (6 sts)
Round 2: ch1, [1 sc, inc] 3 times, slst to join. (9 sts)
Round 3: ch1, [2 sc, inc] 3 times, slst to join. (12 sts)
Round 4: ch1, 1 sc in each st around, slst to join.
Round 5: ch1, 5 sc, dec, 5 sc, slst to join. (11 sts)
Round 6: ch1, 5 sc, 1 3sc-bo (= thumb), 5 sc, slst to join. (11 sts)
Round 7: ch1, 5 sc, dec, 2 sc, dec, slst to join. (9 sts)
Round 8: ch1, 1 sc in each st around, slst to join.
Round 9: ch1, 5 sc, dec, 2 sc, slst to join. (8 sts)
Stuff hand firmly.
Rounds 10–18 (9 rounds): ch1, 1 sc in each st around, slst to join. (8 sts)
Round 19: ch1, 4 sc, dec, 2 sc, change to Marble, slst BLO to join. (7 sts)
Round 20: ch1, 1 sc BLO of each st around, slst to join.
Rounds 21–23 (3 rounds): ch1, 1 sc in each st around, slst to join.
Round 24: ch1, 1 sc in each st around, slst on RS to join.
Stuff the arms lightly halfway.
Flatten out the opening then work 3 sc through both thicknesses at the same time to close.

5 6 7 8 9 10

11

Fasten off and cut, leaving enough yarn for sewing to the body.
Join Blossom yarn to FLO of first st of Round 19 (12), [ch2, slst] 7 times.
Fasten off and weave in ends.
Sew one arm to each side of the body, just below the neck, ensuring that the thumbs are positioned at the front (13, 14).

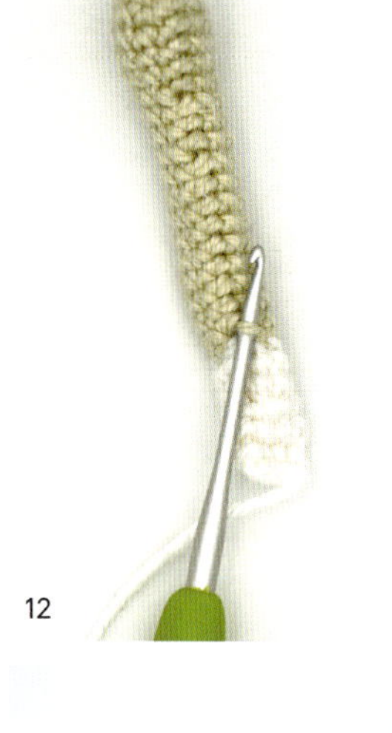
12

13

14

Head

Using Ecru, make MR.
Round 1: 6 sc into MR, slst to join. (6 sts)
Round 2: ch1, inc in each st around, slst to join. (12 sts)
Round 3: ch1, [1 sc, inc] 6 times, slst to join. (18 sts)
Round 4: ch1, [1 sc, inc, 1 sc] 6 times, slst to join. (24 sts)
Round 5: ch1, [3 sc, inc] 6 times, slst to join. (30 sts)
Round 6: ch1, [2 sc, inc, 2 sc] 6 times, slst to join. (36 sts)
Round 7: ch1, [5 sc, inc] 6 times, slst to join. (42 sts)
Round 8: ch1, [3 sc, inc, 3 sc] 6 times, slst to join. (48 sts)
Round 9: ch1, [7 sc, inc] 6 times, slst to join. (54 sts)
Round 10: ch1, [4 sc, inc, 4 sc] 6 times, slst to join. (60 sts)
Round 11: ch1, 1 sc in each st around, slst to join.
Round 12: ch1, [9 sc, inc] 6 times, slst to join. (66 sts)
Round 13: ch1, 1 sc in each st around, slst to join.
Round 14: ch1, 16 sc, inc, 32 sc, inc, 16 sc, slst to join. (68 sts)
Rounds 15–23 (9 rounds): ch1, 1 sc in each st around, slst to join.
Round 24: ch1, 28 sc, ch1, sk 1 st, 10 sc, ch1, sk 1 st, 28 sc, slst to join.
Round 25: ch1, 28 sc, 1 sc into ch, 10 sc, 1 sc into ch, 28 sc, slst to join.

Round 26: ch1, 16 sc, dec, 32 sc, dec, 16 sc, slst to join. (66 sts)
Round 27: ch1, 1 sc in each st around, slst to join.
Round 28: ch1, 15 sc, dec, 32 sc, dec, 15 sc, slst to join. (64 sts)
Insert the eyes into the holes formed by the skipped sts in Round 24.
Round 29: ch1, [14 sc, dec] 4 times, slst to join. (60 sts)
Round 30: ch1, [4 sc, dec, 4 sc] 6 times, slst to join. (54 sts)
Round 31: ch1, [7 sc, dec] 6 times, slst to join. (48 sts)
Round 32: ch1, [4 sc, dec] 8 times, slst to join. (40 sts)
Round 33: ch1, [3 sc, dec] 8 times, slst to join. (32 sts)
Start to stuff.
Round 34: ch1, [2 sc, dec] 8 times, slst to join. (24 sts)
Round 35: ch1, [1 sc, dec] 8 times, slst BLO to join. (16 sts)
Round 36: ch1, 1 sc BLO of each st around, slst to join.
Rounds 37–41 (5 rounds): ch1, 1 sc in each st around, slst to join.
Fasten off and weave in ends. Complete the stuffing.
Push Rounds 36–41 inside the head (15).
Using White floss, embroider the whites of the eyes (16), then add a touch of Brown floss to the sides of the eyes (17).
Using Black floss, embroider the black above the eyes (18) and finish by embroidering the eyelashes (19).
Using the Brown floss, embroider the eyebrows between Rounds 20 and 22 (20).
Using Ecru, embroider the nose between Rounds 26 and 27 (21).
Use a brush and some blush to add a little color to the cheeks and above the nose (21).

15

16

17

18

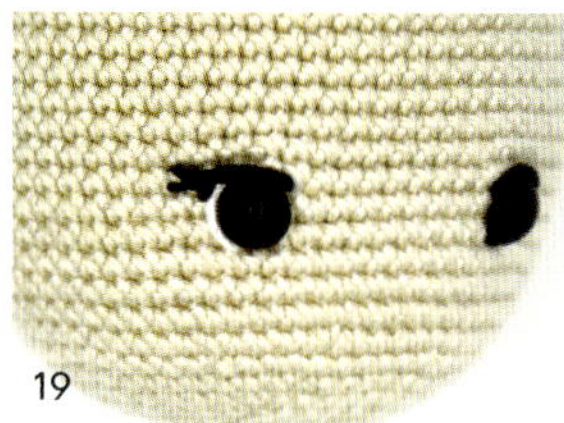
19

20

21

Note: the circumference of the head once stuffed is approximately 7½in (19cm).

EARS (MAKE 2)

Using Ecru, make MR.
Round 1: 1 sc, 4 hdc, 1 sc into MR. (6 sts)
Fasten off, leaving sufficient yarn for sewing to the head.
Sew one ear to each side of the head between Rounds 23 and 27, leaving a gap of 8 sts between ear and eye (22, 23).

ATTACH THE HEAD

Using Ecru, attach the head according to instructions in Techniques: Attaching the Head. Leave 3 rounds in Ecru visible.

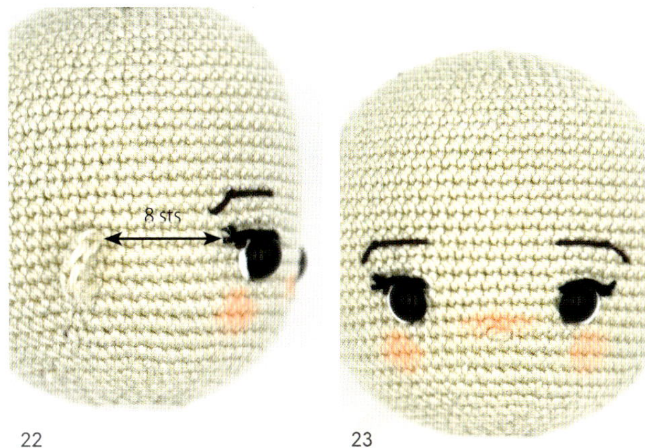

22 23

Hair

PART 1

Using Vanilla, make MR.
Round 1: 6 sc into MR, slst to join. (6 sts)
Round 2: ch1, inc in each st around, slst FLO to join. (12 sts)
Round 3: ch1, [1 sc FLO, inc FLO] 6 times, slst FLO to join. (18 sts)
Round 4: ch1, [1 sc FLO, inc FLO, 1 sc FLO] 6 times, slst to join. (24 sts)
Round 5: ch1, [3 sc, inc] 6 times, slst to join. (30 sts)
Do not cut the yarn and continue with the strands of hair.

Note: it is the WS of the strands of hair that will be visible.

Note: if you are left-handed, reverse the order: start with strand 20 and finish with strand 1.

Strand 1: ch35, and starting in second ch from hook: slst, 33 sc, slst into next st of Round 5 to join.
Strand 2: ch19, and starting in second ch from hook: slst, 1 sc, 16 hdc, slst into next st of Round 5 to join.
Strand 3: ch17, and starting in second ch from hook: slst, 1 sc, 14 hdc, slst into next st of Round 5 to join.
Strand 4: ch15, and starting in second ch from hook: slst, 1 sc, 12 hdc, slst into next st of Round 5 to join.
Strand 5: ch11, and starting in second ch from hook: slst, 1 sc, 8 hdc, slst into next st of Round 5 to join.
Strand 6: ch21, and starting in second ch from hook: slst, 1 sc, 18 hdc, slst into next st of Round 5 to join.
Strand 7: ch23, and starting in second ch from hook: slst, 1 sc, 20 hdc, slst into next st of Round 5 to join.
Strand 8: ch35, and starting in second ch from hook: slst, 33 sc, slst into next st of Round 5 to join.
Strand 9: ch23, and starting in second ch from hook: slst, 1 sc, 20 hdc, slst into next st of Round 5 to join.
Strands 10–19 (10 strands): ch30, and starting in third ch from hook: 28 hdc, sk 1 st, slst into next st of Round 5 to join.
Strand 20: ch17, and starting in second ch from hook: 16 sc, slst into next st of Round 5 to join.
Fasten off and weave in ends (24).

24

PART 2

Join Vanilla yarn to BLO of first st of Round 3 of Part 1 *(25)*.

Note: if you are left-handed, reverse the order: start with strand 12 and finish with strand 1.

Strand 1: ch33, and starting in second ch from hook: slst, 31 sc, slst BLO of next st of Round 3 to join.
Strand 2: ch20, and starting in second ch from hook: slst, 18 sc, slst BLO of next st of Round 3 to join.
Strands 3 and 4 (2 strands): ch18, and starting in second ch from hook: slst, 16 sc, slst BLO of next st of Round 3 to join.
Strand 5: ch33, and starting in second ch from hook: slst, 31 sc, slst BLO of next st of Round 3 to join.
Strands 6–11 (6 strands): ch33, and starting in third ch from hook: 31 hdc, sk 1 st, slst BLO of next st of Round 3 to join.
Strand 12: ch33, and starting in third ch from hook: 31 hdc, slst BLO of next st of Round 3 to join.
Fasten off and weave in ends *(26)*.

PART 3

Join Vanilla yarn to BLO of first st of Round 2 of Part 1 *(27)*.

Note: if you are left-handed, reverse the order: start with strand 8 and finish with strand 1.

Strand 1: ch33, and starting in third ch from hook: 31 hdc, sk 1 st, slst BLO of next st of Round 2.
Strands 2–4 (3 strands): ch80, and starting in second ch from hook: slst, 78 sc, slst BLO of next st of Round 2.
Strands 5–7 (3 strands): ch33, and starting in third ch from hook: 31 hdc, sk 1 st, slst BLO of next st of Round 2.

Strand 8: ch33, and starting in third ch from hook: 31 hdc, slst BLO of first st of Round 2.
Fasten off and weave in ends *(28)*.

ATTACH THE HAIR

Arrange the hair on the head, starting by placing the center of the MR of the hair on the center of the MR of the head. Hold in place with a pin.
Holding Parts 2 and 3 together on top of the head with hair elastic will make things easier.
Part 1: position strands 1–9 and strand 20 on the forehead and the sides *(29–31)*.
Position strands 10–19 around the head *(32)*. It does not matter if there are a few little gaps between the strands – they will be filled in later.
Stick down the strands one by one, applying glue to each strand. Hold in place with pins until the glue has dried.
Part 2: stick strands 2–4 to the forehead *(33)*.
Stick the other strands around the head *(34)*.

25

26

27

28

29

30

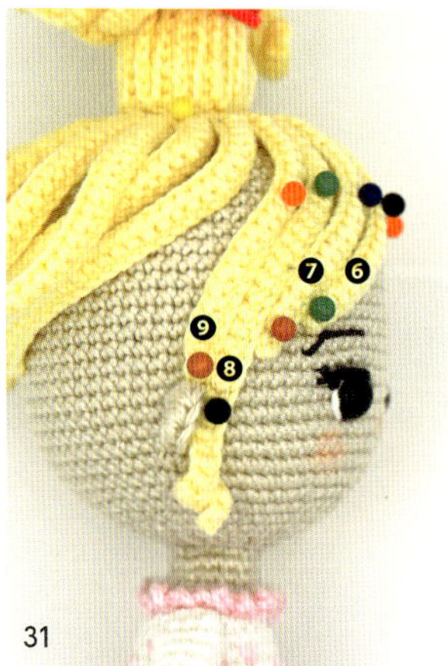

31

32

Part 3: stick all the strands (except strands 2–4) around the head (35).
Pin the 3 remaining strands to the side of the head and plait a braid. Glue the end so it does not come undone (36).
Stick the top of the braid to the head, bringing it a little towards you (37, 38).
Tie a strand of Blossom yarn around the braid (39).

Accessories

RABBIT EARS (MAKE 2)

Note: do not stuff. Work in spiral rounds.

Using Blossom, make MR.
Round 1: 6 sc into MR. (6 sts)
Round 2: [1 sc, inc] 3 times. (9 sts)
Round 3: 1 sc in each st around.
Round 4: [2 sc, inc] 3 times. (12 sts)
Round 5: [3 sc, inc] 3 times. (15 sts)
Round 6: [4 sc, inc] 3 times. (18 sts)
Round 7: 1 sc in each st around.
Round 8: [5 sc, inc] 3 times. (21 sts)
Rounds 9 and 10 (2 rounds): 1 sc in each st around. (21 sts)
Round 11: [5 sc, dec] 3 times. (18 sts)
Round 12: 1 sc in each st around.
Round 13: [4 sc, dec] 3 times. (15 sts)
Round 14: 1 sc in each st around.
Round 15: [3 sc, dec] 3 times. (12 sts)
Rounds 16 and 17 (2 rounds): 1 sc in each st around.
Fasten off, leaving sufficient yarn for sewing to the head.
Fold the base of the ear and sew (40).
Sew the ears to the top of the head (41–43).

MAGIC WAND

Note: work in spiral rounds.

Using Peony Pink, make MR.
Round 1: 5 sc into MR. (5 sts)
Round 2: inc in each st around. (10 sts)
Cut the yarn and work an invisible finish.
Repeat Rounds 1 and 2, but do not cut the yarn. Bring the pieces together as follows:
Round 3: 10 sc into first piece, 10 sc into second piece. (20 sts)
Round 4: 1 sc in each st around.
Round 5: [3 sc, dec] 4 times. (16 sts)
Round 6: [2 sc, dec] 4 times. (12 sts)
Round 7: [1 sc, dec] 4 times. (8 sts)
Stuff.
Round 8: dec 4 times. (4 sts)

33 34 35 36 37 38 39 40 41 42 43

Cut the yarn and fasten off.
Using Peony Pink, close the hole between the 2 "bumps" of the heart (44).
Using Marble, embroider a little "comma" on the side of the heart (45).
Apply some glue to one end of a toothpick and insert into the heart (46).
Wind the Marble yarn around the toothpick, gluing as you go, leaving one end free (47).

44

45

46

47

Shoes (make 2)

SOLES

Using Peony Pink, make the soles according to instructions in Standard Parts: Soles of the Shoes.

MAIN BODY OF SHOE

Join Peony Pink yarn to BLO of third slst of previous round (48).
Round 1: 25 sc BLO, slst to join. (25 sts)
Round 2: ch1, 1 sc in each st around, slst to join.
Round 3: ch1, 9 sc, 3 hdc, 3 dc, 3 hdc, 7 sc, slst to join.
Round 4: ch1, 9 sc, dec twice, 1 sc, dec twice, 7 sc, slst to join. (21 sts)
Round 5: ch1, 7 sc, 10 slst, 4 sc.
Round 6: 7 slst, ch10, sk 10 sts, 4 sc.
Fasten off and weave in ends (49).

48

49

50

51

The Little Companions

BIG COMPANION

Body

Using Peony Pink, work the body according to instructions for the big body in Standard Parts: The Little Companions.

Ears (make 2)

Note: work the ears along a foundation chain for Row 1 and as an oval in Round 2.

Using Peony Pink, ch11 and start in second ch from hook.
Row 1: 3 sc into same st, 9 sc, ch1, turn. (12 sts)
Round 2: 1 sc, 1 hdc, 7 dc, dc-inc 3 times to pass to other side of chain, 7 dc, 1 hdc, 1 sc. (24 sts)
Fasten off, leaving sufficient yarn for sewing to to body.
Fold the base of the ear in half and sew (50).
Sew the ears to the top of the body (51).
Add some blush under the eyes (52).

52

53

Tail

Using Pearl, ch10.
Roll up the chain to form a circle and sew into place (53).
Sew the tail to the back, offset from center (54, 55).

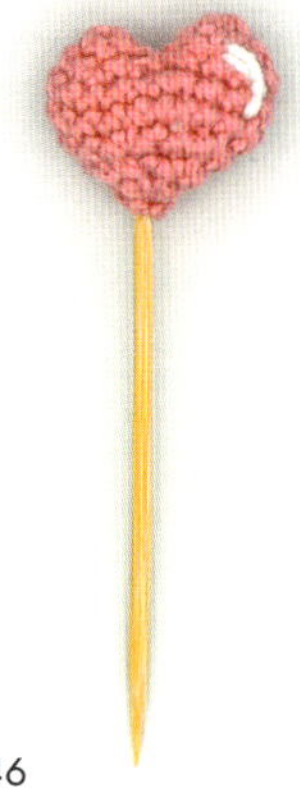

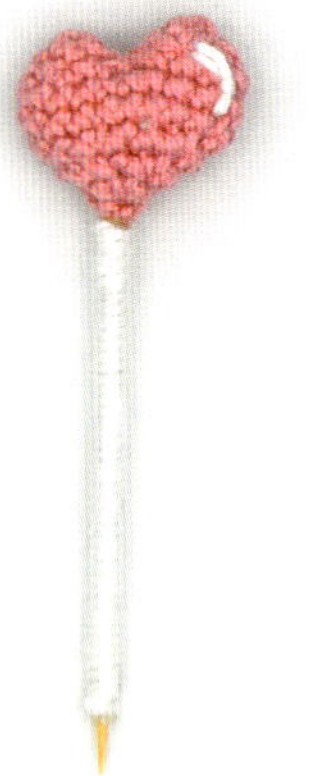

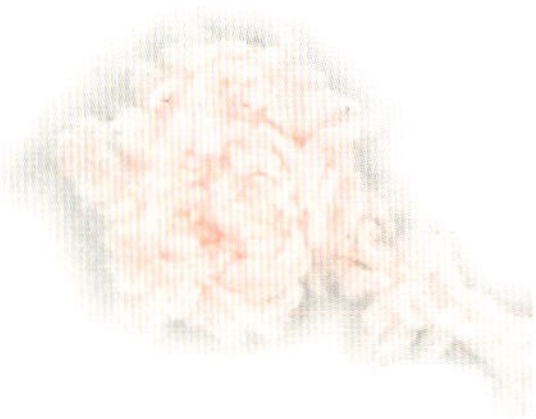

54

55

MEDIUM-SIZED COMPANION

Body

Using Blossom, work the body according to instructions for the medium-sized body in Standard Parts: The Little Companions.

Ears (make 2)

Note: work the ears along a foundation chain for Row 1 and as an oval in Round 2.

Using Blossom, ch10 and start in second ch from hook.
Row 1: 3 sc into same st, 8 sc, ch1, turn. (11 sts)
Round 2: 1 sc, 1 hdc, 6 dc, dc-inc 3 times to pass to other side of chain, 6 dc, 1 hdc, 1 sc. (22 sts)
Fasten off, leaving sufficient yarn for sewing to body.
Fold the base of the ear in half and sew.
Sew the ears to the top of the body.
Add some blush under the eyes.

Tail

Using Pearl, ch10.
Roll up the chain to form a circle and sew into place.
Sew the tail to the back, offset from center *(56)*.

56

57

SMALL COMPANION

Body

Using Marble, work the body according to instructions for the small body in Standard Parts: The Little Companions.

Ears (make 2)

Note: work the ears along a foundation chain for Row 1 and as an oval in Round 2.

Using Marble, ch9 and start in second ch from hook.
Row 1: 3 sc into same st, 7 sc, ch1, turn. (10 sts)
Round 2: 1 sc, 1 hdc, 5 dc, dc-inc 3 times to pass to other side of foundation chain, 5 dc, 1 hdc, 1 sc. (20 sts)
Fasten off, leaving sufficient yarn for sewing together.
Fold the base of the ear in half and sew.
Sew the ears to the top of the body.
Add some blush under the eyes.

Tail

Using Pearl, ch10.
Roll up the chain to form a circle and sew into place.
Sew the tail to the back, offset from center *(57)*.

Akari

Akari lives among the flowers where she cares for her little companions. She loves jumping from flower to flower while twirling her pretty skirt.

Finished Size

Akari: approx 8½in (21.5cm) tall
Companions: between 2¼in (6cm) and 3in (7.5cm) tall

Note :
Size may vary depending on your gauge (tension) and the yarn used

Tools and Materials

Yarn and Colors Must-Have yarn in the following colors:

US 4 (2.00mm) crochet hook
Fiberfill stuffing
2 x 7mm safety eyes
Basic tool kit
(see Materials)

Instructions

Note: always use X-shaped stitches and joined rounds, unless stated otherwise.

Legs (make 2)

Using Pepper, make MR.
Round 1: 6 sc into MR, slst to join. (6 sts)
Round 2: ch1, inc in each st around, slst to join. (12 sts)
Round 3: ch1, [1 sc, inc] 6 times, slst to join. (18 sts)
Rounds 4 and 5 (2 rounds): ch1, 1 sc in each st around, slst to join.
Round 6: ch1, 6 sc, dec 3 times, 6 sc, slst to join. (15 sts)
Round 7: ch1, 5 sc, dec, 1 sc, dec, 5 sc, slst to join. (13 sts)
Rounds 8–12 (5 rounds): ch1, 1 sc in each st around, slst to join.
Round 13: ch1, 2 sc, inc, 7 sc, inc, 2 sc, change to Limestone, slst BLO to join. (15 sts)
Round 14: ch1, 1 sc BLO of each st around, slst to join.
Rounds 15 and 16 (2 rounds): ch1, 1 sc in each st around, slst to join.
Round 17: ch1, 2 sc, dec, 7 sc, dec, 2 sc, slst to join. (13 sts)
Round 18: ch1, 2 sc, inc, 7 sc, inc, 2 sc, slst to join. (15 sts)
Stuff the foot.
Round 19: ch1, 3 sc, inc, 7 sc, inc, 3 sc, slst to join. (17 sts)
Round 20: ch1, 1 sc in each st around, slst to join.
Round 21: ch1, 4 sc, inc, 7 sc, inc, 4 sc, slst to join. (19 sts)
Round 22: ch1, 1 sc in each st around, slst to join.
Round 23: ch1, 5 sc, inc, 7 sc, inc, 5 sc, slst to join. (21 sts)

Round 24: ch1, 1 sc in each st around, slst to join.
Round 25: ch1, 1 sc in each st around, change to Black, slst to join.
Round 26: ch1, 1 sc in each st around, slst to join.
Round 27: ch1, 1 sc in each st around, slst on RS to join.
Mark last slst.
Leg 1: fasten off and weave in ends.
Stuff leg firmly.
Holding the leg with the foot uppermost, join White yarn FLO of first st of Round 13 *(1)*, [ch2, slst] 15 times.
Fasten off and weave in ends *(2)*.
Using Black, embroider little French knots on the sock *(3)*.
Set aside.
Leg 2: repeat steps as for leg 1, but at the end, join with slst on WS.
Stuff leg firmly. Do not mark last slst, do not cut yarn. Continue as follows:

Body

Note: see Diagram 2, Techniques: Joining the Legs.

Round 28: ch1, 8 sc into leg 2, ch2, [1 sc into fourth st before marked slst, 3 sc, 1 sc into same st as marked slst, 16 sc] on leg 1, 2 sc into ch2 and 13 sc into remaining sts of leg 2, slst to join. (46 sts)
Round 29: ch1, 8 sc into leg 2, 2 sc in opposite side of ch2, then [dec, 21 sc] on leg 1, and dec, 11 sc on remaining sts of leg 2, slst to join. (44 sts)

Note: stuff as you go along.

Rounds 30–33 (4 rounds): ch1, 1 sc in each st around, slst to join.
Round 34: ch1, 1 sc in each st around, work an additional 10 sc in order to start next round in middle of back, slst to join. (44 sts)
Round 35: ch1, 14 sc, dec, 11 sc, dec, 15 sc, slst to join. (42 sts)
Round 36: ch1, 1 sc in each st around, slst to join.
Round 37: ch1, 13 sc, dec, 11 sc, dec, 14 sc, slst to join. (40 sts)
Round 38: ch1, 1 sc in each st around, slst to join.
Round 39: ch1, [8 sc, dec] 4 times, slst to join. (36 sts)
Round 40: ch1, 1 sc in each st around, change to Pepper.
Round 41: 1 sc BLO of each st around, slst BLO to join. (36 sts)
Round 42: ch1, 1 sc BLO of each st around, slst to join.
Round 43: ch1, [7 sc, dec] 4 times, slst to join. (32 sts)
Round 44: ch1, 1 sc in each st around, slst to join.
Round 45: ch1, [6 sc, dec] 4 times, slst to join. (28 sts)
Round 46: ch1, 1 sc in each st around, slst to join.
Round 47: ch1, [5 sc, dec] 4 times, slst to join. (24 sts)
Round 48: ch1, 1 sc in each st around, slst to join.

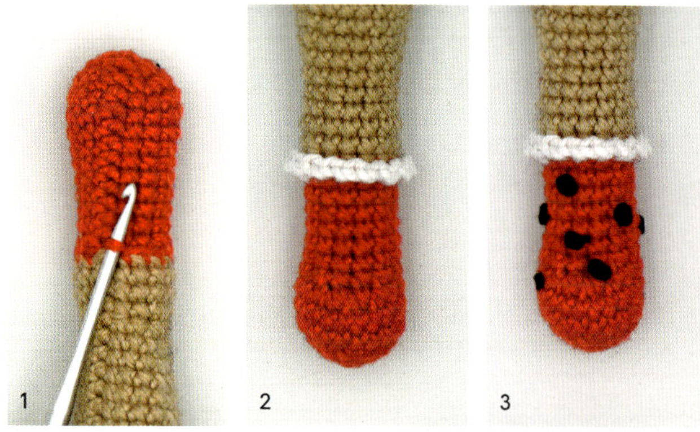

1 2 3

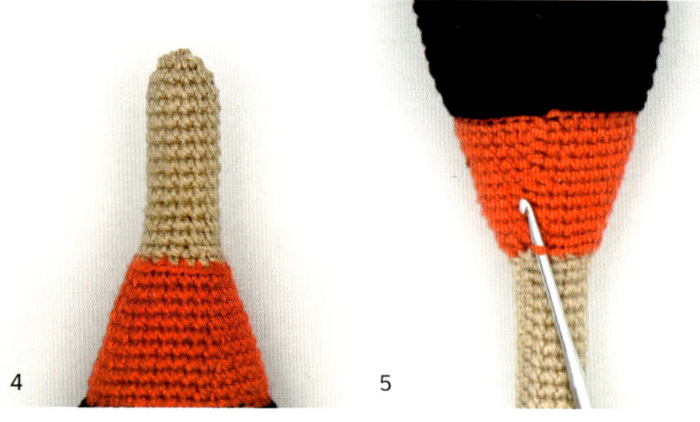

4 5

Round 49: ch1, 6 sc, dec, 10 sc, dec, 4 sc, slst to join. (22 sts)
Round 50: ch1, 1 sc in each st around, slst to join.
Round 51: ch1, 5 sc, dec, 9 sc, dec, 4 sc, change to Limestone, slst BLO to join. (20 sts)
Round 52: ch1, [3 sc BLO, dec BLO] 4 times, slst to join. (16 sts)
Round 53: ch1, [3 sc, dec] twice, 4 sc, dec, slst to join. (13 sts)
Rounds 54–64 (11 rounds): ch1, 1 sc in each st around, slst to join.
Round 65: ch1, 5 sc, dec, 6 sc, slst to join. (12 sts)

Note: strengthen the neck (see Techniques: Strengthening the Neck).

Round 66: ch1, dec 6 times, slst to join. (6 sts)
Cut the yarn and fasten off (4).

Collar

Holding the body neck down, join White yarn to FLO of first st of Round 51 (5).
Round 1: [1 sc FLO, inc FLO] 10 times. (30 sts)
Round 2: 8 hdc, 2 dc, 2 slst, 2 dc, 16 hdc, slst to join.
Cut the yarn and sew down the 2 points of the collar (6).
Using Black, embroider little French knots on the top of the bodice (7).

Skirt

Part 1 (make 21)

Note: work part 1 along a foundation chain.

Using White, ch15 and start in second ch from hook.
Row 1: slst, 1 sc, 1 hdc, 8 dc, 1 hdc, 1 sc, slst to join. (14 sts)
Fasten off, leaving sufficient yarn for sewing together (8).
Repeat until you have 21 pieces (make additional pieces if necessary).
Sew each piece around the body between Rounds 37 and 38 (9, 10)

Part 2 (make 22)

Using Pepper, repeat part 1 until you have 22 pieces (make additional pieces if necessary).
Sew each piece around the body between Rounds 37 and 38 (11).

6 7 8 9

10

11

Arms (make 2)

Using Limestone, make MR.
Round 1: 6 sc into MR, slst to join. (6 sts)
Round 2: ch1, [1 sc, inc] 3 times, slst to join. (9 sts)
Round 3: ch1, [2 sc, inc] 3 times, slst to join. (12 sts)
Round 4: ch1, 1 sc in each st around, slst to join.
Round 5: ch1, 5 sc, dec, 5 sc, slst to join. (11 sts)
Round 6: ch1, 5 sc, 1 3sc-bo (= thumb), 5 sc, slst to join.
Round 7: ch1, 5 sc, dec, 2 sc, dec, slst to join. (9 sts)
Round 8: ch1, 1 sc in each st around, slst to join.
Round 9: ch1, 5 sc, dec, 2 sc, slst to join. (8 sts)
Stuff hand firmly.
Rounds 10–18 (9 rounds): ch1, 1 sc in each st around, slst to join. (8 sts)
Round 19: ch1, 4 sc, dec, 2 sc, change to Pepper, slst BLO to join. (7 sts)
Round 20: ch1, 1 sc BLO of each st around, slst to join.
Rounds 21–23 (3 rounds): ch1, 1 sc in each st around, slst to join.
Round 24: ch1, 1 sc in each stitch, slst on RS to join.
Stuff the arms lightly halfway.
Flatten out the opening, then work 3 sc through both thicknesses at the same time to close.
Fasten off and cut, leaving enough yarn for sewing to body.
Join White yarn to FLO of first st of Round 19 *(12)*. [ch2, slst] 7 times.
Fasten off and weave in ends.
Sew one arm to each side of the body, just below the neck, ensuring that the thumbs are positioned at the front *(13, 14)*.

Head

Using Limestone, make MR.
Round 1: 6 sc into MR, slst to join. (6 sts)
Round 2: ch1, inc in each st around, slst to join. (12 sts)
Round 3: ch1, [1 sc, inc] 6 times, slst to join. (18 sts)
Round 4: ch1, [1 sc, inc, 1 sc] 6 times, slst to join. (24 sts)
Round 5: ch1, [3 sc, inc] 6 times, slst to join. (30 sts)
Round 6: ch1, [2 sc, inc, 2 sc] 6 times, slst to join. (36 sts)
Round 7: ch1, [5 sc, inc] 6 times, slst to join. (42 sts)
Round 8: ch1, [3 sc, inc, 3 sc] 6 times, slst to join. (48 sts)
Round 9: ch1, [7 sc, inc] 6 times, slst to join. (54 sts)
Round 10: ch1, [4 sc, inc, 4 sc] 6 times, slst to join. (60 sts)
Round 11: ch1, 1 sc in each st around, slst to join.
Round 12: ch1, [9 sc, inc] 6 times, slst to join. (66 sts)
Round 13: ch1, 1 sc in each st around, slst to join.
Round 14: ch1, 16 sc, inc, 32 sc, inc, 16 sc, slst to join. (68 sts)
Rounds 15–23 (9 rounds): ch1, 1 sc in each st around, slst to join.
Round 24: ch1, 28 sc, ch1, sk 1 st, 10 sc, ch1, sk 1 st, 28 sc, slst to join. (68 sts)
Round 25: ch1, 28 sc, 1 sc into ch, 10 sc, 1 sc into ch, 28 sc, slst to join. (68 sts)
Round 26: ch1, 16 sc, dec, 32 sc, dec, 16 sc, slst to join. (66 sts)
Round 27: ch1, 1 sc in each st around, slst to join. (66 sts)
Round 28: ch1, 15 sc, dec, 32 sc, dec, 15 sc, slst to join. (64 sts)

12

13

14

15

16

17

18

19

20

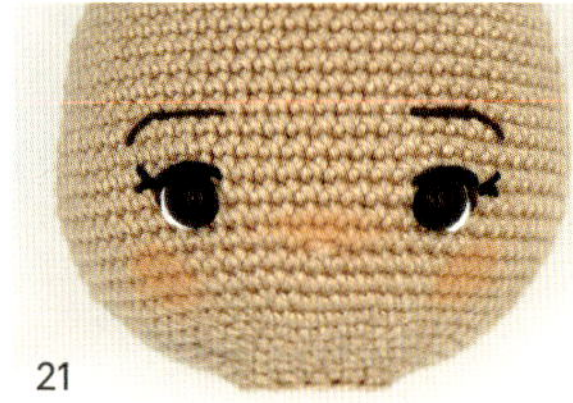
21

22

23

Insert the eyes into the holes formed by the skipped sts in Round 24.
Round 29: ch1, [14 sc, dec] 4 times, slst to join. (60 sts)
Round 30: ch1, [4 sc, dec, 4 sc] 6 times, slst to join. (54 sts)
Round 31: ch1, [7 sc, dec] 6 times, slst to join. (48 sts)
Round 32: ch1, [4 sc, dec] 8 times, slst to join. (40 sts)
Round 33: ch1, [3 sc, dec] 8 times, slst to join. (32 sts)
Start to stuff.
Round 34: ch1, [2 sc, dec] 8 times, slst to join. (24 sts)
Round 35: ch1, [1 sc, dec] 8 times, slst BLO to join. (16 sts)
Round 36: ch1, 1 sc BLO of each st around, slst to join. (16 sts)
Rounds 37–41 (5 rounds): ch1, 1 sc in each st around, slst to join. (16 sts)
Fasten off and weave in ends. Complete the stuffing.
Push Rounds 36–41 inside the head *(15)*.
Using White floss, embroider the whites of the eyes *(16)*, then add a touch of Brown floss to the sides of the eyes *(17)*.
Using Black floss, embroider the black above the eyes *(18)* and finish by embroidering the eyelashes *(19)*.
Using Brown floss, embroider the eyebrows between Rounds 20 and 22 *(20)*.
Using Limestone, embroider the nose between Rounds 26 and 27. Use a brush and some blush to add a little color to the cheeks and above the nose *(21)*.

Note: the circumference of the head once stuffed is approximately 7½in (19cm).

EARS (MAKE 2)

Using Limestone, make MR.
Round 1: 1 sc, 4 hdc, 1 sc into MR. (6 sts)
Fasten off, leaving sufficient yarn for sewing to head.
Sew one ear to each side of the head between Rounds 23 and 27, leaving a gap of 8 sts between ear and eye *(22, 23)*.

ATTACH THE HEAD

Using Limestone, attach the head according to instructions in Techniques: Attaching the Head. Leave 3 rounds in Limestone visible.

24

Hair

PART 1

Using Brunet, make MR.
Round 1: 6 sc into MR, slst to join. (6 sts)
Round 2: ch1, inc in each st around, slst FLO to join. (12 sts)
Round 3: ch1, [1 sc FLO, inc FLO] 6 times, slst FLO to join. (18 sts)
Round 4: ch1, [1 sc FLO, inc FLO, 1 sc FLO] 6 times, slst to join. (24 sts)
Round 5: ch1, [3 sc, inc] 6 times, slst to join. (30 sts)
Do not cut the yarn and continue with the strands of hair.

Note: it is the WS of the strands of hair that will be visible.

Strand 1: ch27, and starting in second ch from hook: slst, 1 sc, 24 hdc, sk 1 st, slst into next st of Round 5 to join.
Strand 2: ch24, and starting in second ch from hook: slst, 1 sc, 21 hdc, sk 1 st, slst into next st of Round 5 to join.
Strand 3: ch21, and starting in second ch from hook: slst, 1 sc, 18 hdc, sk 1 st, slst into next st of Round 5 to join.
Strands 4–7 (4 strands): ch16, and starting in second ch from hook: slst, 1 sc, 13 hdc, sk 1 st, slst into next st of Round 5 to join.
Strand 8: ch21, and starting in second ch from hook: slst, 1 sc, 18 hdc, sk 1 st, slst into next st of Round 5 to join.
Strand 9: ch24, and starting in second ch from hook: slst, 1 sc, 21 hdc, sk 1 st, slst into next st of Round 5 to join.
Strand 10: ch27, and starting in second ch from hook: slst, 1 sc, 24 hdc, sk 1 st, slst into next st of Round 5 to join.
Strands 11–15 (5 strands): ch30, and starting in second ch from hook: slst, 1 sc, 27 hdc, sk 1 st, slst into next st of Round 5 to join.
Fasten off and weave in ends *(24)*.

25

26

27

PART 2

Join Brunet yarn to BLO of first st of Round 3 of Part 1 *(25)*.
Strands 1–3 (3 strands): ch33, and starting in second ch from hook: slst, 31 sc, slst BLO of next st of Round 3 to join.
Strands 4–8 (5 strands): ch19, and starting in second ch from hook: slst, 17 sc, slst BLO of next st of Round 3 to join.
Strands 9–18 (10 strands): ch33, and starting in second ch from hook: slst, 31 sc, slst BLO of next st of Round 3 to join.
Fasten off and weave in ends *(26)*.

PART 3

Join Brunet yarn to BLO of first st of Round 2 of Part 1 *(27)*.
Strands 1–12 (12 strands): ch36, and starting in second ch from hook: slst, 34 sc, slst BLO of next st of Round 2 to join.
Fasten off and weave in ends *(28)*.

ATTACH THE HAIR

Arrange the hair on the head, starting by placing the center of the MR of the hair on the center of the MR of the head. Hold in place with a pin.
Holding Parts 2 and 3 together on top of the head with hair elastic will make things easier.
Part 1: position strands 1–3 and 8–10 in front of the ears *(29)*.
Position strands 4–7 on the forehead *(30)*.
Place all the remaining strands around the head *(31)*. It does not matter if there are a few little gaps between the strands – they will be filled in later. Stick down the strands one by one, applying glue to each strand.
Hold in place with pins until the glue has dried.
Part 2: stick strands 4–8 to the forehead *(32)*.
Stick the other strands around the head *(33)*.
Part 3: stick all the strands around the head *(34, 35)*.

28

29

30

31

32

33

34

35

36

Accessories

ANTENNAE (MAKE 2)

Note: work the antennae along a foundation chain.

Using Black, ch29 and start in second ch from hook.
Row 1: slst in each st of chain. (28 sts)
Fasten off, leaving sufficient yarn for sewing to head.
Sew the antennae to the top of the head and roll up the ends, stiffening with glue if desired (36, 37).

37

FLOWERS (MAKE 6)

Using Sunflower, make MR.
Round 1: 5 sc into MR, change to White, slst to join. (5 sts)
Round 2: ch1, [(1 hdc, 2 dc, 1 hdc) into same st, slst into next st] 5 times.
Fasten off and weave in ends (38).
Stick one flower on the hair (39).

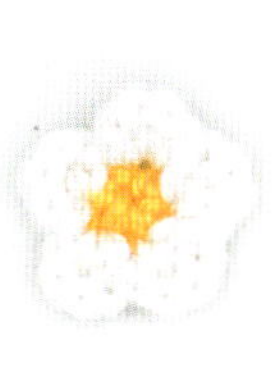
38

39

Shoes (make 2)

SOLES

Using Pepper, make the soles according to instructions in Standard Parts: Soles of the Shoes.

MAIN BODY OF SHOE

Join Black yarn to BLO of third slst of previous round (40).
Round 1: 25 sc BLO, slst to join. (25 sts)
Round 2: ch1, 1 sc in each st around, slst to join. (25 sts)
Round 3: ch1, 9 sc, 3 hdc, 3 dc, 3 hdc, 7 sc, slst to join. (25 sts)
Round 4: ch1, 9 sc, dec twice, 1 sc, dec twice, 7 sc, slst to join. (21 sts)
Round 5: ch1, 7 sc, 10 slst, 4 sc. (21 sts)
Round 6: 7 slst, ch10, sk 10 sts, 4 sc. (21 sts)
Fasten off and weave in ends (41).

40

41

The Little Companions

BIG COMPANION

Body

Using Black, work the body according to instructions for the big body in Standard Parts: The Little Companions.
Embroider the eyes in white.

Antennae (make 2)

Note: work the antennae along a foundation chain.

Using Black, ch21 and start in second ch from hook.
Row 1: slst in each st of chain. (20 sts)
Fasten off, leaving sufficient yarn for sewing to body.
Sew the antennae to the top of the body and roll up the ends, stiffening with glue if desired (42).

Wings (make 2)

Note: work the wings in ovals around a foundation chain.

Using Pepper, ch11 and start in second ch from hook.
Round 1: 1 sc, 1 hdc, 6 dc, 1 hdc, (1 sc, ch2, 1 sc) into last ch to pass to other side of foundation chain, 1 hdc, 6 dc, 1 hdc, 1 sc, ch2. (24 sts)
Cut the yarn and work an invisible finish (43).
Repeat Round 1 but do not cut the yarn.
Using Black, embroider French knots on the second piece (44).

Lay one piece on top of the other, and work 24 sc all the way round, working into both pieces together (45, 46).
Fasten off, leaving sufficient yarn for sewing to body.
Make another identical wing.
Sew the wings to the back of the body (47, 48).

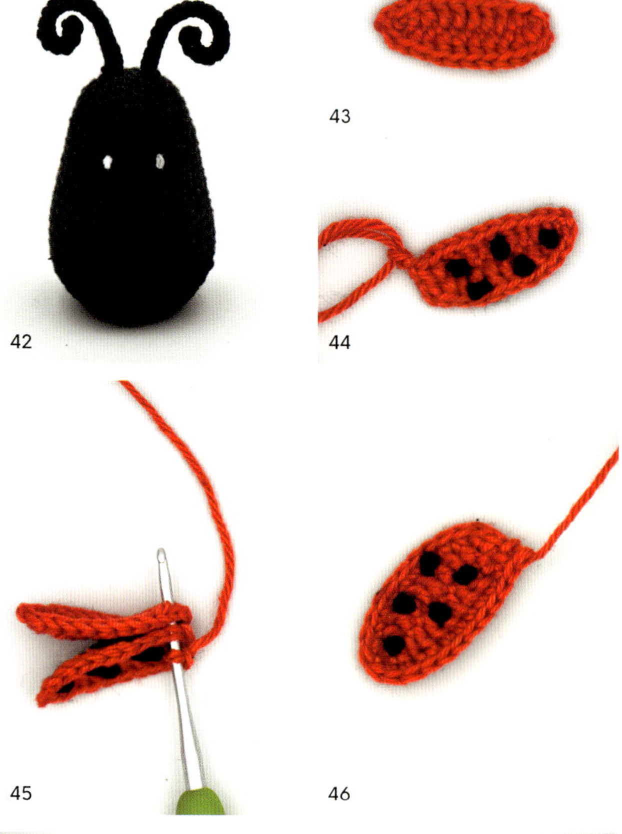
42 43 44 45 46

47

48

MEDIUM-SIZED COMPANION

Body

Using Black, work the body according to instructions for the medium-sized body in Standard Parts: The Little Companions. Embroider the eyes in white.

Antennae (make 2)

Note : work the antennae along a foundation chain.

Using Black, ch19 and start in second ch from hook.
Row 1: slst in each st of chain. (18 sts)
Fasten off, leaving sufficient yarn for sewing to body.
Sew the antennae to the top of the head and roll up the ends, stiffening with glue if desired.

Wings (make 2)

Using Pepper, work as for big companion's wings.
Sew the wings to the back of the body (49).

SMALL COMPANION

Body

Using Black, work the body according to instructions for the small body in Standard Parts: The Little Companions. Embroider the eyes in white.

Antennae (make 2)

Note: work the antennae along a foundation chain.

Using Black, ch17 and start in second ch from hook.
Row 1: slst in each st of chain. (6 sts)
Fasten off, leaving sufficient yarn for sewing to body.
Sew the antennae to the top of the head and roll up the ends, stiffening with glue if desired.

Wings (make 2)

Using Pepper, work as for big companion's wings.
Sew the wings to the back of the body (50).

49

50

Difficulty: ● ● ●

Karin

Join Karin and her little companions for a very special game! This one includes pompoms full of sweets, and a little imagination.

Finished Size

Karin: approx 9in (23cm) tall
Companions: between 1½in (4cm) and 2¾in (7cm) tall

Note :
Size may vary depending on your gauge (tension) and the yarn used

Tools and Materials

Yarn and Colors Must-Have yarn in the following colors:

Yarn and Colors Furry yarn in the following color:

US 4 (2.00mm) crochet hook
Fiberfill stuffing
2 x 7mm safety eyes
Basic tool kit
(see Materials)

Instructions

Note: always use X-shaped stitches and joined rounds, unless stated otherwise.

Legs (make 2)

Using Must-Have Pastel Pink, make MR.
Round 1: 6 sc into MR, slst to join. (6 sts)
Round 2: ch1, inc in each st around, slst to join. (12 sts)
Round 3: ch1, [1 sc, inc] 6 times, slst to join. (18 sts)
Rounds 4 and 5 (2 rounds): ch1, 1 sc in each st around, slst to join.
Round 6: ch1, 6 sc, dec 3 times, 6 sc, slst to join. (15 sts)
Round 7: ch1, 5 sc, dec, 1 sc, dec, 5 sc, slst to join. (13 sts)
Round 8: ch1, 1 sc in each st around, change to Light Pink, slst to join.
Round 9: ch1, 1 sc in each st, slst to join.
Round 10: ch1, 1 sc in each st around, change to Pastel Pink, slst to join.
Round 11: ch1, 1 sc in each st around, slst to join.
Round 12: ch1, 1 sc in each st around, change to Light Pink, slst to join.
Round 13: ch1, 2 sc, inc, 7 sc, inc, 2 sc, slst to join. (15 sts)
Round 14: ch1, 1 sc in each st around, change to Pastel Pink, slst to join.
Round 15: ch1, 1 sc in each st around, slst to join.
Round 16: ch1, 1 sc in each st around, change to Light Pink, slst to join.

Round 17: ch1, 2 sc, dec, 7 sc, dec, 2 sc, slst to join. (13 sts)
Round 18: ch1, 2 sc, inc, 7 sc, inc, 2 sc, change to Pastel Pink, slst to join. (15 sts)
Stuff the foot.
Round 19: ch1, 3 sc, inc, 7 sc, inc, 3 sc, slst to join. (17 sts)
Round 20: ch1, 1 sc in each st around, change to Light Pink, slst to join.
Round 21: ch1, 4 sc, inc, 7 sc, inc, 4 sc, slst to join. (19 sts)
Round 22: ch1, 1 sc in each st around, change to Limestone.
Round 23: 1 sc BLO of each st around, slst BLO to join.
Round 24: ch1, 5 sc BLO, inc BLO, 7 sc BLO, inc BLO, 5 sc BLO, slst to join. (21 sts)
Rounds 25 and 26 (2 rounds): ch1, 1 sc in each st around, slst to join.
Round 27: ch1, 1 sc in each st around, change to White, slst.
Round 28: ch1, 1 sc in each st around, slst on RS to join.
Mark last slst.
Leg 1: fasten off and weave in ends.
Stuff leg firmly.
Leg 2: repeat steps as for leg 1, but at end, slst into last st on WS.
Stuff leg firmly. Do not mark last slst, do not cut yarn, but continue as follows:

Body

Note: see Diagram 2, Techniques: Joining the Legs.

Round 29: ch1, 8 sc into leg 2, ch2, then [1 sc into fourth st before marked slst, 3 sc, 1 sc into same st as marked slst, 16 sc] on leg 1, 2 sc into ch2 and 13 sc into remaining sts of leg 2, slst to join. (46 sts)
Round 30: ch1, 8 sc into leg 2, 2 sc in opposite side of ch2, then [dec, 21 sc] on leg 1, and dec, 11 sc on remaining sts of leg 2, slst to join. (44 sts)

Note: stuff as you go along.

Rounds 31–34 (4 rounds): ch1, 1 sc in each st around, slst to join.
Round 35: ch1, 1 sc in each st around, work an additional 10 sc in order to start next round in middle of back, slst to join.
Round 36: ch1, 14 sc, dec, 11 sc, dec, 15 sc, slst to join. (42 sts)
Round 37: ch1, 1 sc in each st around, slst to join.
Round 38: ch1, 13 sc, dec, 11 sc, dec, 14 sc, slst to join. (40 sts)
Round 39: ch1, 1 sc in each st around, slst to join.
Round 40: ch1, [8 sc, dec] 4 times, slst to join. (36 sts)
Rounds 41 and 42 (2 rounds): ch1, 1 sc in each st around, slst to join.
Round 43: ch1, [7 sc, dec] 4 times, slst to join. (32 sts)
Round 44: ch1, 1 sc in each st around, change to Light Pink, slst BLO to join.
Round 45: ch1, [6 sc BLO, dec BLO] 4 times, slst BLO to join. (28 sts)
Round 46: ch1, 1 sc BLO of each st around, slst to join.
Round 47: ch1, [5 sc, dec] 4 times, slst to join. (24 sts)
Round 48: ch1, 1 sc in each st around, slst to join.
Round 49: ch1, 6 sc, dec, 10 sc, dec, 4 sc, change to Limestone, slst BLO to join. (22 sts)
Round 50: ch1, 1 sc BLO of each st around, slst to join.
Round 51: ch1, 5 sc, dec, 9 sc, dec, 4 sc, slst to join. (20 sts)
Round 52: ch1, [3 sc, dec] 4 times, slst to join. (16 sts)
Round 53: ch1, [3 sc, dec] twice, 4 sc, dec, slst to join. (13 sts)
Rounds 54–64 (11 rounds): ch1, 1 sc in each st around, slst to join.
Round 65: ch1, 5 sc, dec, 6 sc, slst to join. (12 sts)

Note: strengthen the neck: see Techniques: strengthing the neck.

Round 66: ch1, dec 6 times, slst to join. (6 sts)
Cut the yarn and fasten off (1).
Holding the body neck down, join Lemon yarn to FLO of first st of Round 49 (2).
Round 1: (ch1, 1 sc, ch1, 1 sc) into same st, (ch1, 1 sc, ch1, 1 sc) into next st 21 times.
Fasten off and weave in ends (3).

Dress

Holding the body, neck down, join White yarn to FLO of first st on back of Round 44 (4).

Round 1: 32 sc FLO, slst to join. (32 sts)
Round 2: ch1, [7 hdc, hdc-inc] 4 times, slst to join. (36 sts)
Round 3: ch1, 1 hdc in each st, slst to join.
Round 4: ch1, [8 hdc, hdc-inc] 4 times, slst to join. (40 sts)
Round 5: ch1, 1 hdc in each st, slst to join.
Round 6: ch1, 13 hdc, hdc-inc, 12 hdc, hdc-inc, 13 hdc, slst to join. (42 sts)
Round 7: ch1, 1 hdc in each st, slst to join.
Round 8: ch1, 13 hdc, hdc-inc, 14 hdc, hdc-inc, 13 hdc, slst to join. (44 sts)
Rounds 9–11 (3 rounds): ch1, 1 hdc in each st, slst to join.
Round 12: ch1, 1 hdc in each st around, change to Lemon, slst BLO to join.
Round 13: ch1, hdc-inc BLO in each st around, slst to join. (88 sts)
Round 14: ch1, hdc-inc in each st around, slst to join. (176 sts)
Fasten off and weave in ends (5).
Holding the body neck down, join Must-Have Pastel Pink yarn to FLO of first st of Round 45 of body (6).
Round 1: (1 sc, 1 hdc, 1 dc) FLO of same st, (1 dc, 1 hdc, 1 sc) FLO of next st, 1 sc, [(1 sc, 1 hdc, 1 dc) FLO of next st, (1 dc, 1 hdc, 1 sc) FLO of next st, 1 slst] 8 times, 1 slst. (64 sts)
Round 2: [ch3, sk 2 sts, 1 sc, ch3, sk 2 sts, 1 sc, slst] 9 times, slst to join.
Fasten off and weave in ends (7).

HEART

Using Must-Have Pastel Pink, make MR.
Round 1: ch2, 2 hdc, 1 sc, ch2, 1 sc, 2 hdc, ch2, slst into MR.
Fasten off, leaving sufficient yarn for sewing to the dress (8).
Sew the heart to the dress (9).

Arms (make 2)

Using Limestone, make MR.
Round 1: 6 sc into MR, slst to join. (6 sts)
Round 2: ch1, [1 sc, inc] 3 times, slst to join. (9 sts)
Round 3: ch1, [2 sc, inc] 3 times, slst to join. (12 sts)
Round 4: ch1, 1 sc in each st around, slst to join.
Round 5: ch1, 5 sc, dec, 5 sc, slst to join. (11 sts)
Round 6: ch1, 5 sc, 1 3sc-bo (= thumb), 5 sc, slst to join.
Round 7: ch1, 5 sc, dec, 2 sc, dec, slst to join. (9 sts)
Round 8: ch1, 1 sc in each st around, slst to join.
Round 9: ch1, 5 sc, dec, 2 sc, slst to join. (8 sts)
Stuff hand firmly.
Rounds 10–18 (9 rounds): ch1, 1 sc in each st around, slst to join.
Round 19: ch1, 4 sc, dec, 2 sc, slst to join. (7 sts)
Rounds 20–23 (4 rounds): ch1, 1 sc in each st around, slst to join.
Round 24: ch1, 1 sc in each st around, slst on RS to join.
Stuff the arms lightly halfway.
Flatten out the opening, then work 3 sc through both thicknesses at the same time to close.
Fasten off and cut, leaving enough yarn for sewing to body.

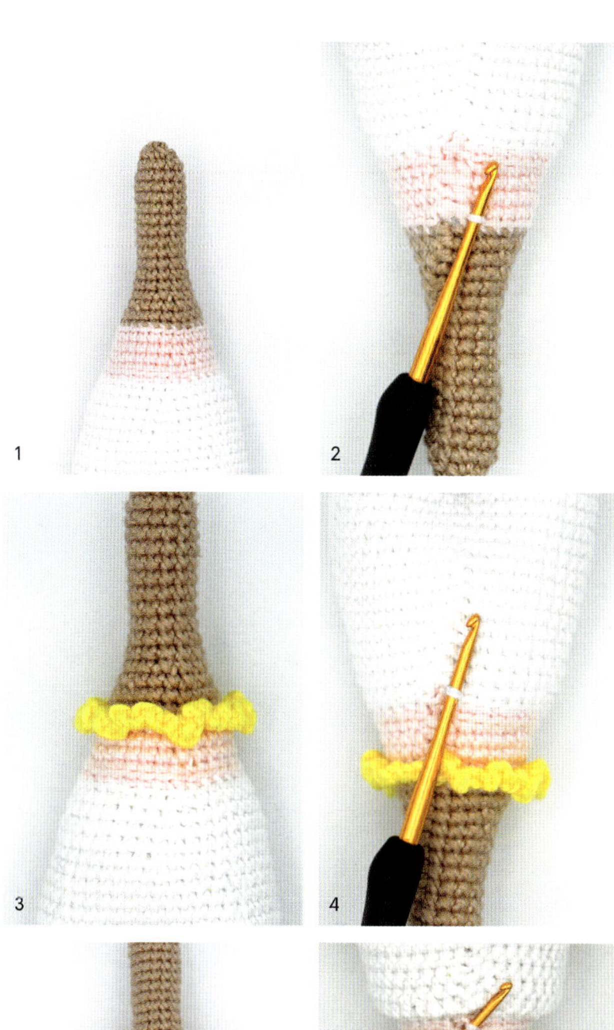
1 2 3 4

5

6 7

8

9

Wrap a strand of Lemon yarn and a strand of White yarn around one wrist *(10)*.

Sew one arm to each side of the body, 2 rounds above the neckline, ensuring that the thumbs are positioned at the front *(11, 12)*.

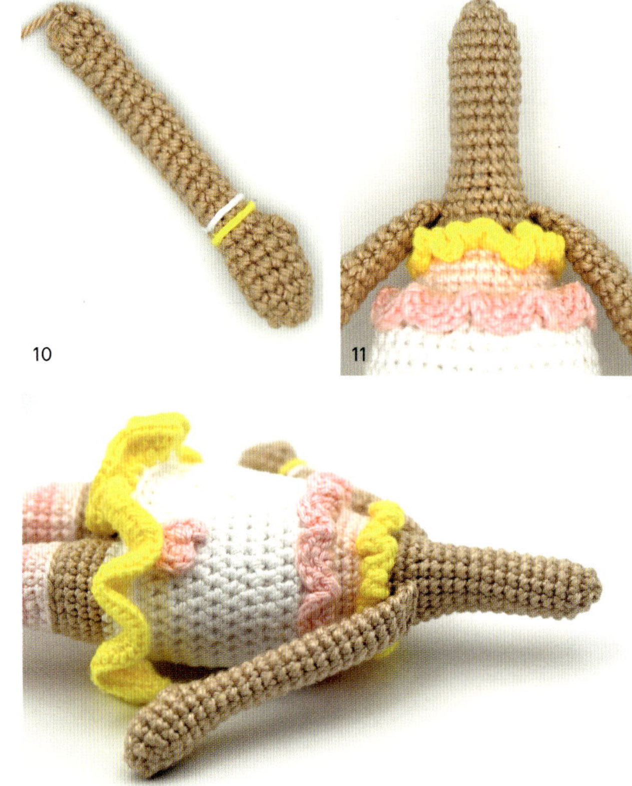

10

11

12

Head

Using Limestone, make MR.

Round 1: 6 sc into MR, slst to join. (6 sts)

Round 2: ch1, inc in each st around, slst to join. (12 sts)

Round 3: ch1, [1 sc, inc] 6 times, slst to join. (18 sts)

Round 4: ch1, [1 sc, inc, 1 sc] 6 times, slst to join. (24 sts)

Round 5: ch1, [3 sc, inc] 6 times, slst to join. (30 sts)

Round 6: ch1, [2 sc, inc, 2 sc] 6 times, slst to join. (36 sts)

Round 7: ch1, [5 sc, inc] 6 times, slst to join. (42 sts)

Round 8: ch1, [3 sc, inc, 3 sc] 6 times, slst to join. (48 sts)

Round 9: ch1, [7 sc, inc] 6 times, slst to join. (54 sts)

Round 10: ch1, [4 sc, inc, 4 sc] 6 times, slst to join. (60 sts)

Round 11: ch1, 1 sc in each st around, slst to join.

Round 12: ch1, [9 sc, inc] 6 times, slst to join. (66 sts)

Round 13: ch1, 1 sc in each st around, slst to join.

Round 14: ch1, 16 sc, inc, 32 sc, inc, 16 sc, slst to join. (68 sts)

Rounds 15–23 (9 rounds): ch1, 1 sc in each st around, slst to join.

Round 24: ch1, 28 sc, ch1, sk 1 st, 10 sc, ch1, sk 1 st, 28 sc, slst to join.

Round 25: ch1, 28 sc, 1 sc into ch, 10 sc, 1 sc into ch, 28 sc, slst to join. (68 sts)

Round 26: ch1, 16 sc, dec, 32 sc, dec, 16 sc, slst to join. (66 sts)

Round 27: ch1, 1 sc in each st around, slst to join.

Round 28: ch1, 15 sc, dec, 32 sc, dec, 15 sc, slst to join. (64 sts)

Insert the eyes into the holes formed by the skipped sts in Round 24.

Round 29: ch1, [14 sc, dec] 4 times, slst to join. (60 sts)

Round 30: ch1, [4 sc, dec, 4 sc] 6 times, slst to join. (54 sts)

Round 31: ch1, [7 sc, dec] 6 times, slst to join. (48 sts)

Round 32: ch1, [4 sc, dec] 8 times, slst to join. (40 sts)

Round 33: ch1, [3 sc, dec] 8 times, slst to join. (32 sts)

Start to stuff.

Round 34: ch1, [2 sc, dec] 8 times, slst to join. (24 sts)

Round 35: ch1, [1 sc, dec] 8 times, slst BLO to join. (16 sts)

Round 36: ch1, 1 sc BLO of each st around, slst to join.

Rounds 37–41 (5 rounds): ch1, 1 sc in each st around, slst to join. (16 sts)

Fasten off and weave in ends. Complete the stuffing.

Push Rounds 36–41 inside the head *(13)*.

Using White floss, embroider the whites of the eyes *(14)*, then add a touch of Blue floss to the sides of the eyes *(15)*.

Using Black floss, embroider the black above the eyes and finish by embroidering the eyelashes *(16)*.

Using the Brown floss, embroider the eyebrows between Rounds 20 and 22 *(17)*.

Using Limestone, embroider the nose between Rounds 26 and 27. Use a brush and some blush to add a little color to the cheeks and above the nose *(18)*.

Note: the circumference of the head once stuffed is approximately 7½in (19cm).

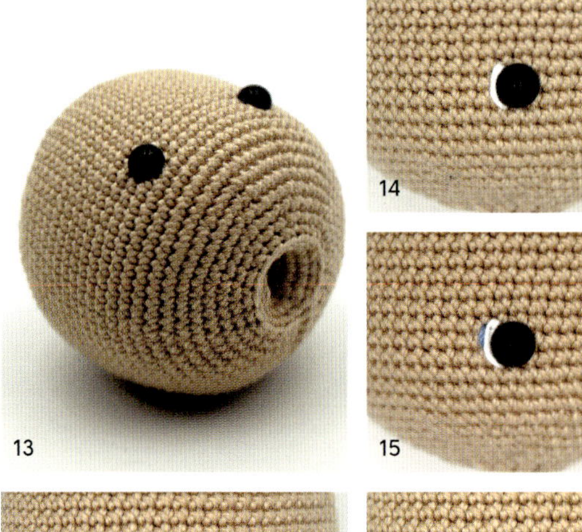

13

14

15

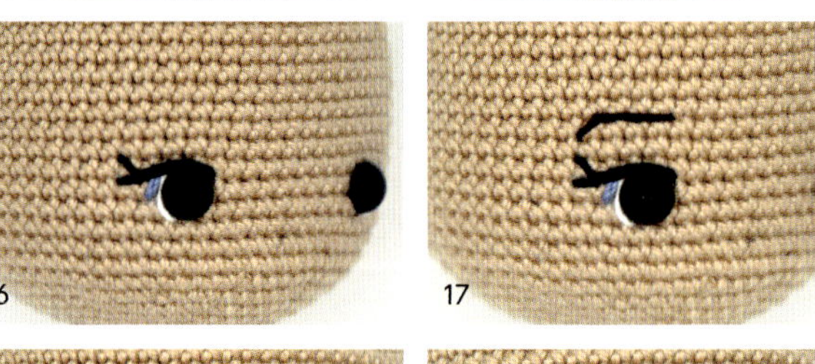

16

17

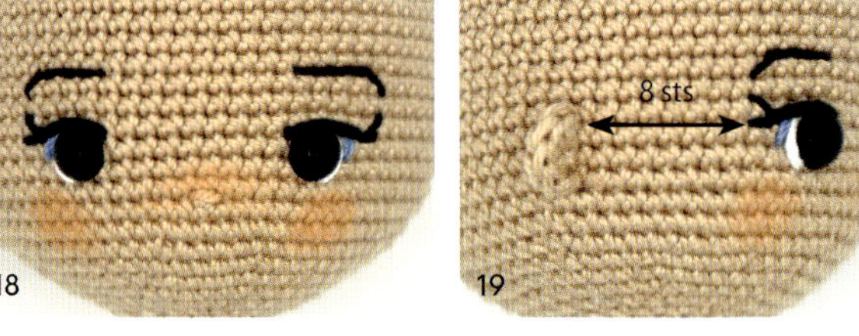

18

19

EARS (MAKE 2)

Using Limestone, make MR.
Round 1: 1 sc, 4 hdc, 1 sc into MR. (6 sts)
Fasten off, leaving sufficient yarn for sewing to head.
Sew one ear to each side of the head between Rounds 23 and 27, leaving a gap of 8 sts between ear and eye *(19, 20)*.

ATTACH THE HEAD

Using Limestone, attach the head according to instructions in Techniques: Attaching the Head.
Leave 6 rounds in Limestone visible.

Hair

PART 1

Using Caramel, make MR.
Round 1: 6 sc into MR, slst to join. (6 sts)
Round 2: ch1, inc in each st around, slst to join. (12 sts)
Round 3: ch1, [1 sc, inc] 6 times, slst to join. (18 sts)
Round 4: ch1, [1 sc, inc, 1 sc] 6 times, slst to join. (24 sts)
Round 5: ch1, [3 sc, inc] 6 times, slst to join. (30 sts)
Do not cut the yarn. Continue with the strands of hair.

Note: it is the WS of the strands of hair that will be visible.

Strand 1: ch31, and starting in second ch from hook: slst, 1 sc, 3 hdc into the next st, 1 hdc, 3 hdc into next st, 1 hdc, hdc-inc, 21 hdc, 1 sc, slst, slst into next st of Round 5 to join.
Strand 2: ch21, and starting in second ch from hook: slst, 1 sc, 16 hdc, 1 sc, slst, slst into next st of Round 5 to join.
Strands 3–11 (9 strands): ch16, and starting in second ch from hook: slst, 1 sc, 11 hdc, 1 sc, slst, slst into next st of Round 5 to join.
Strand 12: ch21, and starting in second ch from hook: slst, 1 sc, 16 hdc, 1 sc, slst, slst into next st of Round 5 to join.
Strand 13: ch31, and starting in second ch from hook: slst, 1 sc, 3 hdc into next st, 1 hdc, 3 hdc into next st, 1 hdc, hdc-inc, 21 hdc, 1 sc, slst, slst into next st of Round 5 to join.
Strands 14–30 (17 strands): ch28, and starting in third ch from hook: 24 hdc, 1 sc, slst, slst into next st of Round 5 to join.
Fasten off and weave in ends *(21)*.

ATTACH THE HAIR

Arrange the hair on the head, starting by placing the center of the MR of the hair on the center of the MR of the head. Hold in place with a pin.
Position strands 1, 2, 12, and 13 in front of the ears *(22, 23)*.
Position strands 3–11 on the forehead *(24)*.
Arrange the remaining strands around the head *(25)*.
Stick down the strands one by one, applying glue to each strand. Hold in place with pins until the glue has dried.

20 21

22

23

24

25

TOPKNOT

Note: work in spiral rounds.

Using Caramel, make MR.
Round 1: 6 sc into MR. (6 sts)
Round 2: inc BLO of each st around. (12 sts)
Round 3: [1 sc BLO, inc BLO] 6 times. (18 sts)
Round 4: [1 sc BLO, inc BLO, 1 sc BLO] 6 times. (24 sts)
Round 5: [3 sc BLO, inc BLO] 6 times. (30 sts)
Round 6: [2 sc BLO, inc BLO, 2 sc BLO] 6 times. (36 sts)
Round 7: [5 sc BLO, inc BLO] 6 times. (42 sts)
Round 8: [3 sc BLO, inc BLO, 3 sc BLO] 6 times. (48 sts)
Rounds 9–11 (3 rounds): 1 sc BLO of each st around.
Round 12: [3 sc BLO, dec BLO, 3 sc BLO] 6 times. (42 sts)
Round 13: [5 sc BLO, dec BLO] 6 times. (36 sts)
Round 14: 1 sc BLO of each st around.
Fasten off and cut, leaving enough yarn for sewing to hair.
Join Caramel yarn to FLO of first st of Round 1 *(26)*, [ch5, 1 sc] FLO of each st of Rounds 1–13.
Fasten off and weave in ends *(27)*.
Stuff.
Sew the topknot to the top of the head *(28)*.

26 27 28 29 30

Accessories

ELASTIC

Using Must-Have Pastel Pink, ch48.
Fasten off and cut, leaving enough yarn for sewing together.

Sew the chain around the topknot *(29)*.
Using Must-Have Pastel Pink, make MR.
Round 1: ch2, 2 hdc, 1 sc, ch2, 1 sc, 2 hdc, ch2, slst into MR.
Fasten off and cut, leaving enough yarn for sewing together.
Sew the heart to the side of the topknot *(30)*.
Using White, embroider 1 French knot on each ear *(31)*.

CAT EARS (MAKE 2)

Note: work in spiral rounds.

Using Must-Have Pastel Pink, make MR.
Round 1: 4 sc into MR. (4 sts)
Round 2: inc in each st around. (8 sts)
Round 3: [1 sc, inc] 4 times. (12 sts)
Round 4: [2 sc, inc] 4 times. (16 sts)
Rounds 5–7 (3 rounds): 1 sc in each st around.
Fasten off and cut, leaving enough yarn for sewing together.
Using Light Pink, embroider the inside of the ear (32).
Sew one ear to each side of the head (33, 34).

31 32 33

34

Shoes (make 2)

SOLES

Using Must-Have Pastel Pink, make the soles according to instructions in Standard Parts: Soles of the Shoes.

MAIN BODY OF SHOE (MAKE 2)

Join Must-Have Pastel Pink yarn to BLO of third slst of previous round (35).
Round 1: 25 sc BLO, slst to join. (25 sts)
Rounds 2 and 3 (2 rounds): ch1, 1 sc in each st around, slst to join.
Round 4: ch1, 7 sc, [1 hdc, 1 hdc-dec] 4 times, 1 hdc, 5 sc, change to Lemon. (21 sts)
Round 5: slst in each st around.
Round 6: [ch2, slst BLO] 21 times.
Fasten off and weave in ends (36).

35 36

The Little Companions

BIG COMPANION

Body

Using Must-Have Pastel Pink, work the body according to instructions for the big body in Standard Parts: The Little Companions.

Ears (make 2)

Note: work in spiral rounds.

Using Must-Have Pastel Pink, make MR.
Round 1: 6 sc into MR. (6 sts)
Round 2: [1 sc, inc] 3 times. (9 sts)
Round 3: [2 sc, inc] 3 times. (12 sts)
Rounds 4 and 5 (2 rounds): 1 sc in each st around.
Fasten off and cut, leaving enough yarn for sewing to body.
Using Light Pink, embroider the inside of the ear (37).
Sew one ear to each side of thebody between Rounds 2 and 7 (38).

37 38

Details

Using Light Pink, embroider 2 lines on each side between rounds 13 and 16 *(39)*, and 3 lines on the top of the body between Rounds 1 and 4 *(40)*.

Tail

Note: work in spiral rounds.

Using Must-Have Pastel Pink, make MR.
Round 1: 6 sc into MR. (6 sts)
Rounds 2–16 (15 rounds): 1 sc in each st around.
Flatten out the opening, then work 3 sc through both thicknesses at the same time to close.
Fasten off, leaving sufficient yarn for sewing to body.
Sew the tail to the back of the body between Rounds 19 and 23 *(41)*.
Add some blush under the eyes *(42)*.

MEDIUM-SIZED COMPANION

Body

Using Light Pink, work the body according to instructions for the medium-sized body in Standard Parts: The Little Companions.

Ears (make 2)

Note: work in spiral rounds.

Using Light Pink, make MR.
Round 1: 5 sc into MR. (5 sts)
Round 2: [1 sc, inc] twice, 1 sc. (7 sts)
Round 3: [inc, 2 sc] twice, 1 sc. (9 sts)
Round 4: 1 sc in each st around.
Fasten off and cut, leaving enough yarn for sewing to body.
Using White, embroider the inside of the ear.
Sew one ear to each side of the head between Rounds 2 and 7.

Details

Using White, embroider 2 lines on each side between Rounds 11 and 14, and 3 lines on the top of the head between Rounds 1 and 4.

Tail

Note: work in spiral rounds.

Using Light Pink, make MR.
Round 1: 6 sc into MR. (6 sts)
Rounds 2–14 (13 rounds): 1 sc in each st around.
Flatten out the opening, then work 3 sc through both thicknesses at the same time to close.
Fasten off, leaving sufficient yarn for sewing together.
Sew the tail to the back of the body between Rounds 15 and 18.
Add some blush under the eyes *(43)*.

39 40

41

42

43

SMALL COMPANION

Body

Using White, work the body according to instructions for the small body in Standard Parts: The Little Companions.

Ears (make 2)

Note: work in spiral rounds.

Using White, make MR.
Round 1: 4 sc into MR. (4 sts)
Round 2: [1 sc, inc] twice. (6 sts)
Round 3: [2 sc, inc] twice. (8 sts)
Fasten off and cut, leaving enough yarn for sewing to body.
Using Light Pink, embroider the inside of the ear.
Sew one ear to each side of the body between Rounds 2 and 7.

Details

Using Light Pink, embroider 2 lines on each side between Rounds 11 and 14, and 3 lines on the top of the body between Rounds 1 and 4.

Tail

Note: work in spiral rounds.

Using White, make MR.
Round 1: 6 sc into MR. (6 sts)
Rounds 2–12 (11 rounds): 1 sc in each st around.
Flatten out the opening, then work 3 sc through both thicknesses at the same time to close.
Fasten off, leaving sufficient yarn for sewing to body.
Sew the tail to the back of body between Rounds 13 and 16.
Add some blush under the eyes (44).

Pompoms (make 3)

Using Furry Pastel Pink, make 3 pompoms in different sizes (45).

44

45

Takane

What is Takane's favorite animal? The giraffe, of course! She loves their elegance and discretion. Living among them with her little companions gives her a sense of serenity.

Finished Size

Takane: approx 8½in (21.5cm) tall
Companions: between 2¼in (6cm) and 2¾in (7cm) tall

Note :
Size may vary depending on your gauge (tension) and the yarn used

Tools and Materials

Yarn and Colors Must-Have yarn in the following colors:

US 4 (2.00mm) crochet hook
Fiberfill stuffing
2 x 7mm safety eyes
Basic tool kit
(see Materials)

Instructions

Note: always use X-shaped stitches and joined rounds, unless stated otherwise.

Legs (make 2)

Using Limestone, make MR.
Round 1: 6 sc into MR, slst to join. (6 sts)
Round 2: ch1, inc in each st around, slst to join. (12 sts)
Round 3: ch1, [1 sc, inc] 6 times, slst to join. (18 sts)
Rounds 4 and 5 (2 rounds): ch1, 1 sc in each st around, slst to join.
Round 6: ch1, 6 sc, dec 3 times, 6 sc, slst to join. (15 sts)
Round 7: ch1, 5 sc, dec, 1 sc, dec, 5 sc, slst to join. (13 sts)
Rounds 8–13 (6 rounds): ch1, 1 sc in each st around, slst to join.
Round 14: ch1, 2 sc, inc, 7 sc, inc, 2 sc, slst to join. (15 sts)
Rounds 15–17 (3 rounds): ch1, 1 sc in each st around, slst to join.
Round 18: ch1, 2 sc, dec, 7 sc, dec, 2 sc, slst to join. (13 sts)
Round 19: ch1, 2 sc, inc, 7 sc, inc, 2 sc, slst to join. (15 sts)
Stuff the foot.
Round 20: ch1, 3 sc, inc, 7 sc, inc, 3 sc, slst to join. (17 sts)
Round 21: ch1, 1 sc in each st around, slst to join.
Round 22: ch1, 4 sc, inc, 7 sc, inc, 4 sc, slst to join. (19 sts)
Round 23: ch1, 1 sc in each st around, slst to join.
Round 24: ch1, 5 sc, inc, 7 sc, inc, 5 sc, change to Teak, slst to join. (21 sts)
Rounds 25–27 (3 rounds): ch1, 1 sc in each st around, slst to join.

Round 28: ch1, 1 sc in each stitch, slst on RS to join.
Mark last slst.
Leg 1: fasten off and weave in ends.
Stuff leg firmly.
Leg 2: repeat steps as for leg 1, but at end, work last slst on WS. Stuff leg firmly. Do not mark last slst, do not cut yarn. Continue as follows:

Body

Note: see Diagram 2, Techniques: Joining the Legs.

Round 29: ch1, 8 sc into leg 2, ch2, [1 sc into fourth st before marked slst, 3 sc, 1 sc into same st as marked slst, 16 sc] on leg 1, 2 sc into ch2 and 13 sc into remaining sts of leg 2, slst to join. (46 sts)
Round 30: ch1, 8 sc into leg 2, 2 sc in opposite side of ch2, [dec, 21 sc] on leg 1, [dec, 11 sc] on remaining sts of leg 2, slst to join. (44 sts)

Note: stuff as you go along.

Rounds 31–34 (4 rounds): ch1, 1 sc in each st around, slst to join.
Round 35: ch1, 1 sc in each st around, work an additional 10 sc in order to start next round in middle of back, slst to join.
Round 36: ch1, 14 sc, dec, 10 sc, dec, 16 sc, change to Mustard, slst to join. (42 sts)
Round 37: ch1, 1 sc in each st, slst to join.
Round 38: ch1, 13 sc, dec, 10 sc, dec, 15 sc, slst to join. (40 sts)
Round 39: ch1, 1 sc in each st around, slst to join.
Round 40: ch1, [8 sc, dec] 4 times, slst to join. (36 sts)
Rounds 41 and 42 (2 rounds): ch1, 1 sc in each st around, slst to join.
Round 43: ch1, [7 sc, dec] 4 times, slst to join. (32 sts)
Round 44: ch1, 1 sc in each st around, slst to join.
Round 45: ch1, [6 sc, dec] 4 times, slst to join. (28 sts)
Round 46: ch1, 1 sc in each st around, slst to join.
Round 47: ch1, [5 sc, dec] 4 times, slst to join. (24 sts)
Round 48: ch1, 1 sc in each st around, slst to join.
Round 49: ch1, 6 sc, dec, 10 sc, dec, 4 sc, change to Limestone. (22 sts)
Round 50: slst BLO of each st around.
Round 51: 1 sc BLO of each st around, slst to join.
Round 52: ch1, 6 sc, dec, 10 sc, dec, 2 sc, slst to join. (20 sts)
Round 53: ch1, [3 sc, dec] 4 times, slst to join. (16 sts)
Round 54: ch1, [3 sc, dec] twice, 4 sc, dec, slst to join. (13 sts)
Rounds 55–65 (11 rounds): ch1, 1 sc in each st around, slst to join.
Round 66: ch1, 5 sc, dec, 6 sc, slst to join. (12 sts)

Note: strengthen the neck (see Techniques: Strengthening the Neck

Round 67: ch1, dec 6 times, slst to join. (6 sts)
Cut the yarn and fasten off *(1)*.

HEM OF SHORTS (MAKE 2)

Note: work the hems in ovals around a foundation chain. Adjust the number of sts in the foundation chain to the circumference of the leg.

Using Teak, ch26 and start in second ch from hook.
Round 1: 24 sc, 4 sc into last ch to pass to other side of foundation chain, 24 sc. (52 sts)
Fasten off and cut, leaving enough yarn for sewing to legs.
Sew around the leg at the color change *(2)*.

BELT

Note: work the belt in an oval around a foundation chain. Adjust the number of sts in the foundation chain to the waist circumference if necessary.

Using Teak, ch47 and start in third ch from hook.
Round 1: 44 hdc, 4 hdc into same ch to pass to other side of foundation chain, 44 hdc. (92 sts)
Fasten off and cut, leaving enough yarn for sewing to body.
Sew the belt around the body at the color change *(3)*.
Using Black, embroider the belt buckle *(4)*.
Using Teak, embroider the belt loops *(5)*.

SPOTS

Part 1 (make 4)
Using Soil, make MR.
Round 1: 4 sc into MR, slst on RS to join. (4 sts)
Fasten off and weave in ends.
Part 2 (make 4)
Using Soil, make MR.
Round 1: 5 sc into MR, slst on RS to join. (5 sts)
Fasten off and weave in ends.
Sew the spots to the upper part of the body (6).

Arms (make 2)

Using Limestone, make MR.
Round 1: 6 sc into MR, slst to join. (6 sts)
Round 2: ch1, [1 sc, inc] 3 times, slst to join. (9 sts)
Round 3: ch1, [2 sc, inc] 3 times, slst to join. (12 sts)
Round 4: ch1, 1 sc in each st around, slst to join.
Round 5: ch1, 5 sc, dec, 5 sc, slst to join. (11 sts)
Round 6: ch1, 5 sc, 1 3sc-bo (= thumb), 5 sc, slst to join.
Round 7: ch1, 5 sc, dec, 2 sc, dec, slst to join. (9 sts)
Round 8: ch1, 1 sc in each st around, slst to join.
Round 9: ch1, 5 sc, dec, 2 sc, slst to join. (8 sts)
Stuff hand firmly.
Rounds 10–18 (9 rounds): ch1, 1 sc in each st around, slst to join.
Round 19: ch1, 4 sc, dec, 2 sc, change to Mustard. (7 sts)
Round 20: slst BLO of each st around.
Round 21: 1 sc BLO of each st around, slst to join.
Rounds 22 and 23 (2 rounds): ch1, 1 sc in each st around, slst to join.
Round 24: ch1, 1 sc in each st around, change to Limestone.
Round 25: slst BLO of each st around.
Stuff the arms lightly halfway.
Flatten out the opening, then work 3 sc through both thicknesses at the same time to close.
Fasten off and cut, leaving enough yarn for sewing to body.
Using Black, Mustard, and Sapphire, embroider 3 bracelets on one arm (7).
Sew one arm to each side of the body, 2 rounds above the color change, ensuring that the thumbs are positioned at the front (8, 9).

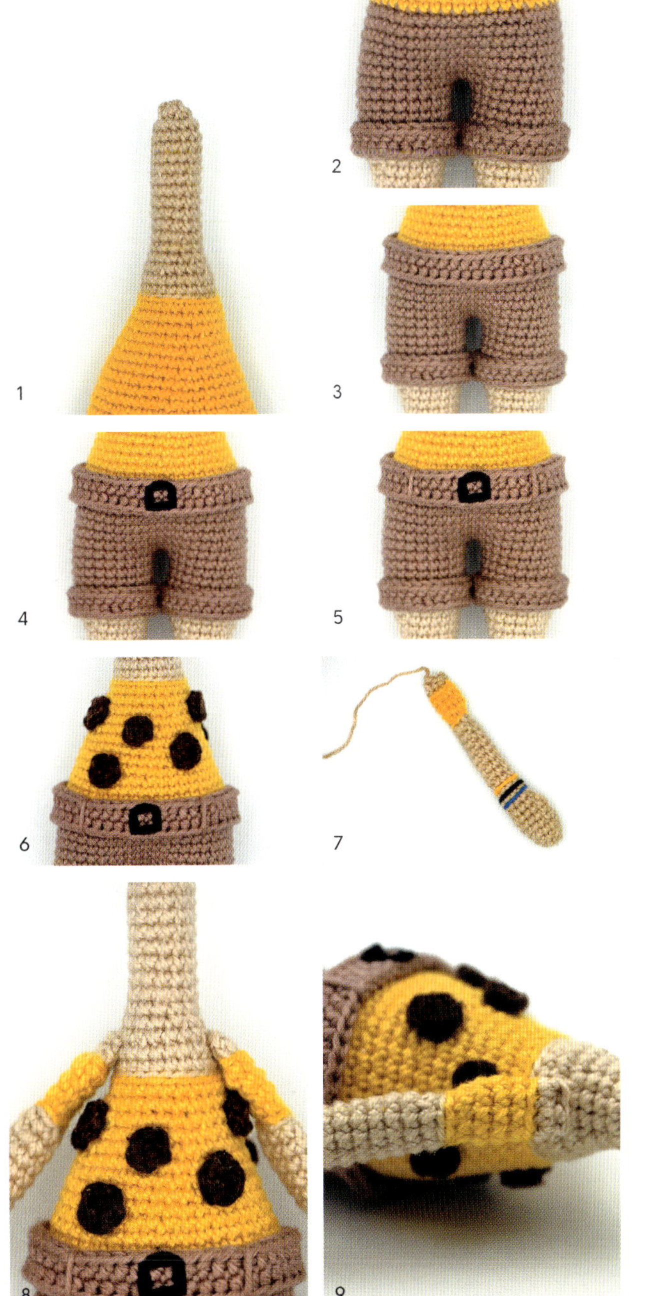

Head

Using Limestone, make MR.
Round 1: 6 sc into MR, slst to join. (6 sts)
Round 2: ch1, inc in each st around, slst to join. (12 sts)
Round 3: ch1, [1 sc, inc] 6 times, slst to join. (18 sts)
Round 4: ch1, [1 sc, inc, 1 sc] 6 times, slst to join. (24 sts)
Round 5: ch1, [3 sc, inc] 6 times, slst to join. (30 sts)
Round 6: ch1, [2 sc, inc, 2 sc] 6 times, slst to join. (36 sts)
Round 7: ch1, [5 sc, inc] 6 times, slst to join. (42 sts)
Round 8: ch1, [3 sc, inc, 3 sc] 6 times, slst to join. (48 sts)
Round 9: ch1, [7 sc, inc] 6 times, slst to join. (54 sts)
Round 10: ch1, [4 sc, inc, 4 sc] 6 times, slst to join. (60 sts)
Round 11: ch1, 1 sc in each st around, slst to join.

Round 12: ch1, [9 sc, inc] 6 times, slst to join. (66 sts)
Round 13: ch1, 1 sc in each st around, slst to join.
Round 14: ch1, 16 sc, inc, 32 sc, inc, 16 sc, slst to join. (68 sts)
Rounds 15–23 (9 rounds): ch1, 1 sc in each st around, slst to join.
Round 24: ch1, 28 sc, ch1, sk 1 st, 10 sc, ch1, sk 1 st, 28 sc, slst to join.
Round 25: ch1, 28 sc, 1 sc into ch, 10 sc, 1 sc into ch, 28 sc, slst to join.
Round 26: ch1, 16 sc, dec, 32 sc, dec, 16 sc, slst to join. (66 sts)
Round 27: ch1, 1 sc in each st around, slst to join.
Round 28: ch1, 15 sc, dec, 32 sc, dec, 15 sc, slst to join. (64 sts)
Insert the eyes into the holes formed by the skipped sts in Round 24.
Round 29: ch1, [14 sc, dec] 4 times, slst to join. (60 sts)
Round 30: ch1, [4 sc, dec, 4 sc] 6 times, slst to join. (54 sts)
Round 31: ch1, [7 sc, dec] 6 times, slst to join. (48 sts)
Round 32: ch1, [4 sc, dec] 8 times, slst to join. (40 sts)
Round 33: ch1, [3 sc, dec] 8 times, slst to join. (32 sts)
Start to stuff.
Round 34: ch1, [2 sc, dec] 8 times, slst to join. (24 sts)
Round 35: ch1, [1 sc, dec] 8 times, slst BLO to join. (16 sts)
Round 36: ch1, 1 sc BLO of each st around, slst to join.
Rounds 37–41 (5 rounds): ch1, 1 sc in each st around, slst to join.
Fasten off and weave in ends. Complete the stuffing.
Push Rounds 36–41 inside the head *(10)*.
Using White floss, embroider the whites of the eyes *(11)*, then add a touch of Blue floss to the sides of the eyes *(12)*.
Using Black floss, embroider the black above the eyes *(13)* and finish by embroidering the eyelashes *(14)*.
Using Brown floss, embroider the eyebrows between Rounds 20 and 22 *(15)*.
Using Limestone, embroider the nose between Rounds 26 and 27. Use a brush and some blush to add a little color to the cheeks and above the nose *(16)*.

Note: the circumference of the head once stuffed is approximately 7½in (19cm).

EARS (MAKE 2)

Using Limestone, make MR.
Round 1: 1 sc, 4 hdc, 1 sc into MR. (6 sts)
Fasten off, leaving sufficient yarn for sewing together.
Sew one ear to each side of the head between Rounds 23 and 27, leaving a gap of 8 sts between ear and eye *(17, 18)*.

ATTACH THE HEAD

Using Limestone, attach the head according to instructions in Techniques: Attaching the Head. Leave 5 rounds in Limestone visible.

NECKLACE

Using Black, Mustard, and Sapphire, embroider the necklace *(19)*.

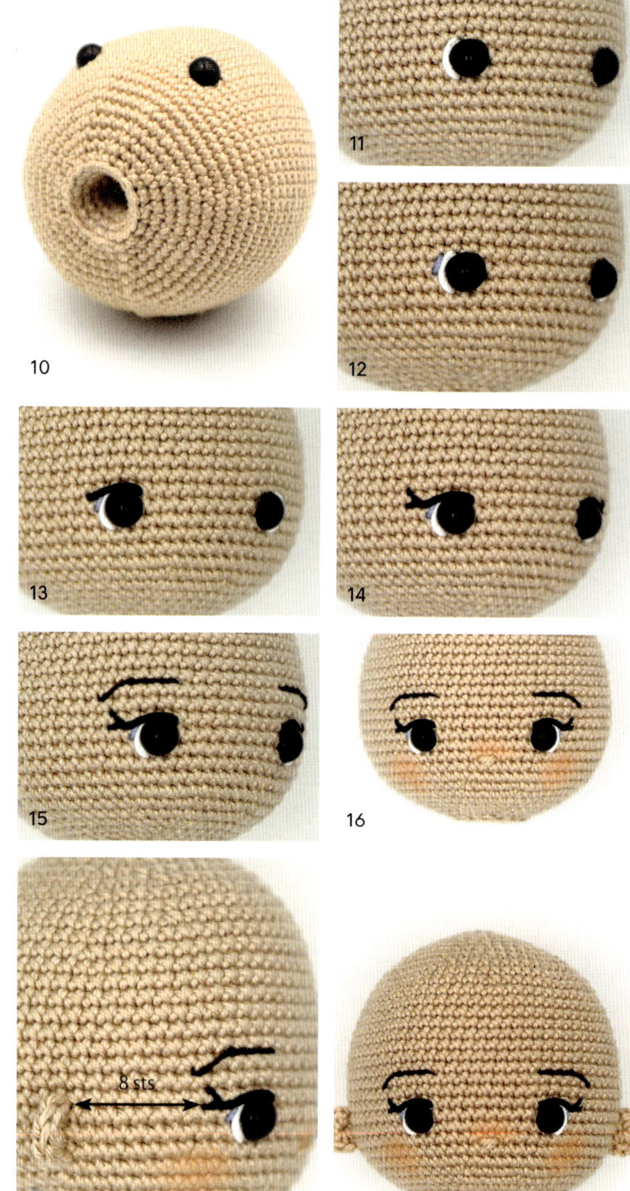

10, 11, 12, 13, 14, 15, 16, 17, 18

19

Hair

PART 1

Using Brunet, make MR.
Round 1: 6 sc into MR, slst to join. (6 sts)
Round 2: ch1, inc in each st around, slst FLO to join. (12 sts)
Round 3: ch1, [1 sc FLO, inc FLO] 6 times, slst FLO to join. (18 sts)
Round 4: ch1, [1 sc FLO, inc FLO, 1 sc FLO] 6 times, slst to join. (24 sts)
Round 5: ch1, [3 sc, inc] 6 times, slst to join. (30 sts)
Do not cut the yarn and continue with the strands of hair.

Note: it is the WS of the strands of hair that will be visible.

Note: if you are left-handed, reverse the order: start with strand 30 and finish with strand 1.

Strand 1: ch45, and starting in second ch from hook: slst, 1 sc, 40 hdc, 1 sc, slst, slst into next st of Round 5 to join.
Strand 2: ch17, and starting in second ch from hook: slst, 1 sc, 12 hdc, 1 sc, slst, slst into next st of Round 5 to join.
Strand 3: ch45, and starting in second ch from hook: slst, 1 sc, 40 hdc, 1 sc, slst, slst into next st of Round 5 to join.
Strand 4: ch25, and starting in third ch from hook: 21 hdc, 1 sc, slst, slst into next st of Round 5 to join.
Strand 5: ch21, and starting in third ch from hook: 17 hdc, 1 sc, slst, slst into next st of Round 5 to join.
Strand 6: ch17, and starting in third ch from hook: 13 hdc, 1 sc, slst, slst into next st of Round 5 to join.
Strand 7: ch13, and starting in third ch from hook: 9 hdc, 1 sc, slst, slst into next st of Round 5 to join.
Strand 8: ch9, and starting in third ch from hook: 5 hdc, 1 sc, slst, slst into next st of Round 5 to join.
Strands 9–25 (17 strands): ch29, and starting in third ch from hook: 25 hdc, 1 sc, slst, slst into next st of Round 5 to join.
Strand 26: repeat strand 8.
Strand 27: repeat strand 7.
Strand 28: repeat strand 6.
Strand 29: repeat strand 5.
Strand 30: repeat strand 4.
Fasten off and weave in ends (20).

PART 2

Join the Brunet yarn to BLO of first st of Round 3 of Part 1 (21).

Note: if you are left-handed, reverse the order: start with strand 18 and finish with strand 1.

Strand 1: ch37, and starting in third ch from hook: 33 hdc, 1 sc, slst, slst BLO of next st of Round 3 to join.
Strand 2: ch15, and starting in second ch from hook: slst, 13 sc, slst BLO of next st of Round 3 to join.
Strand 3: ch37, and starting in third ch from hook: 33 hdc, 1 sc, slst, slst BLO of next st of Round 3 to join.
Strand 4: ch21, and starting in third ch from hook: 17 hdc, 1 sc, slst, slst BLO of next st of Round 3 to join.

20

21

22

Strands 5–8 (4 strands): ch60, and starting in second ch from hook: slst, 1 sc, 55 hdc, 1 sc, slst, slst BLO of next st of Round 3 to join.
Strands 9–13 (5 strands): ch33, and starting in third ch from hook: 29 hdc, 1 sc, slst, slst BLO of next st of Round 3 to join.
Strands 14–17 (4 strands): ch60, and starting in second ch from hook: slst, 1 sc, 55 hdc, 1 sc, slst, slst BLO of next st of Round 3 to join.
Strand 18: ch21, and starting in third ch from hook: 17 hdc, 1 sc, slst, slst BLO of next st of Round 3 to join.
Fasten off and weave in ends (22).

PART 3

Join the Brunet yarn to BLO of first st of Round 2 of Part 1 (23).

Note: if you are left-handed, reverse the order: start with strand 12 and finish with strand 1.

Strand 1: ch39, and starting in third ch from hook: 35 hdc, 1 sc, slst, slst BLO of next st of Round 2.
Strands 2–4 (3 strands): ch62, and starting in second ch from hook: slst, 1 sc, 57 hdc, 1 sc, slst, slst BLO of next st of Round 2 to join.
Strands 5–8 (4 strands): ch35, and starting in third ch from hook: 31 hdc, 1 sc, slst, slst BLO of next st of Round 2 to join.
Strands 9–11 (3 strands): ch62, and starting in second ch from hook: slst, 1 sc, 57 hdc, 1 sc, slst, slst BLO of next st of Round 2 to join.
Strand 12: ch39, and starting in third ch from hook: 35 hdc, 1 sc, slst, slst BLO of next st of Round 2 to join.
Fasten off and weave in ends (24).

23 24 25 26

ATTACH THE HAIR

Arrange the hair on the head, starting by placing the center of the MR of the hair on the center of the MR of the head. Hold in place with a pin.
Holding Parts 2 and 3 together on top of the head with hair elastic will make things easier.
Part 1: position strand 2 on the forehead (25).
Position strands 1 and 3 on each side of the head, in front of the ears (25).
Position strands 4–8 on one side and 26–30 on on the other (26, 27).

Stick down the strands one by one, applying glue to each strand. Hold in place with pins until the glue has dried.
Arrange all the remaining strands around the head (28, 29) and glue into place. It does not matter if there are a few little gaps between the strands – they will be filled in later.
Part 2: glue strand 2 to the forehead (30).
Glue strands 18, 1, 3, and 4 to the sides (30,31).
Glue strands 5–8 and 14–17 to the sides, applying glue down to ear level (32, 33).
Glue the remaining strands to the back of the head (34).
Part 3: stick down strands 1–12 (35).
Glue strands 2–4 and 9–11 to the sides, applying glue down to ear level (36, 37).
Glue the remaining strands to the back of the head (38).
Using Brunet, tie the long strands together to form bunches (39, 40).

27
28
29
30
31
32
33
34
35
36
37
38
39
40

Accessories

GIRAFFE HORNS (MAKE 2)

Note: work in spiral rounds.

Using Soil, make MR.
Round 1: 5 sc into MR. (5 sts)
Round 2: [1 sc, inc] twice, 1 sc. (7 sts)
Round 3: [1 sc, dec] twice, 1 sc. (5 sts)
Change to Mustard.
Rounds 4–7 (4 rounds): 1 sc in each st around.
Fasten off and cut, leaving enough yarn for sewing to head.
Sew the horns to the head *(41, 42)*.

41

42

GIRAFFE EARS (MAKE 2)

Note: work in spiral rounds.

Using Mustard, make MR.
Round 1: 4 sc into MR. (4 sts)
Round 2: 1 sc in each st around.
Round 3: inc in each st around. (8 sts)
Round 4: 1 sc in each st around.
Round 5: [1 sc, inc] 4 times. (12 sts)
Round 6: [2 sc, inc] 4 times. (16 sts)
Round 7: [3 sc, inc] 4 times. (20 sts)
Round 8: 1 sc in each st around.
Round 9: [3 sc, dec] 4 times. (16 sts)
Round 10: [2 sc, dec] 4 times. (12 sts)
Round 11: [1 sc, dec] 4 times. (8 sts)

Fasten off and cut, leaving enough yarn for sewing to head.
Sew one ear to each side of the head
(43, 44).

43

44

Shoes (make 2)

SOLES

Using Black make the soles according to instructions in Standard Parts: Soles of the Shoes.
Sew the 2 soles together using Soil.

MAIN BODY OF SHOE

Join Soil yarn to BLO of third slst of previous round *(45)*.
Round 1: 25 sc BLO, slst to join. (25 sts)
Rounds 2 and 3 (2 rounds): ch1, 1 sc in each st around, slst to join.
Round 4: ch1, 7 sc [1 sc, dec] 4 times, 6 sc, slst to join. (21 sts)
Round 5: ch1, 8 sc, dec, 3 sc, dec, 6 sc, slst to join. (19 sts)
Rounds 6 and 7 (2 rounds): ch1, 1 sc in each st around, slst to join. (19 sts)
Round 8: ch1, 1 sc in each st around, change to Black, slst to join. (19 sts)
Round 9: ch1, 1 sc in each st around, slst on RS to join. (19 sts)
Fasten off and weave in ends.
Using Black, embroider the laces between Rounds 6 and 9 *(46)*.

Bag

Note: work in spiral rounds.

Using Soil, make MR.
Round 1: 6 sc into MR. (6 sts)
Round 2: inc in each st around. (12 sts)
Round 3: [1 sc, inc] 6 times. (18 sts)
Round 4: [1 sc, inc, 1 sc] 6 times. (24 sts)
Rounds 5–8 (4 rounds): 1 sc in each st around.
Round 9: (1 sc, dec, 1 sc) 6 times. (18 sts)
Round 10: [1 sc, dec] 6 times. (12 sts)
Flatten out the opening, then work 6 sc through both thicknesses at the same time to close.
Ch45, then slst at other end of bag to join (47).
Fasten off and weave in ends.

45 46 47 48

The Little Companions

BIG COMPANION

Body

Using Mustard, work the body according to instructions for the big body in Standard Parts: The Little Companions.

Horns (make 2)

Note: work in spiral rounds.

Using Soil, make MR.
Round 1: 4 sc into MR. (4 sts)
Round 2: 1 sc in each st around.
Change to Mustard.
Rounds 3 and 4 (2 rounds): 1 sc in each st around.
Fasten off and cut, leaving enough yarn for sewing to body.
Sew the horns on top of the head between Rounds 1 and 3 (48).

Ears (make 2)

Note: work the ears in ovals around a foundation chain.

Using Mustard, ch6 and start in second ch from hook.
Round 1: slst, 1 sc, 1 hdc, 1 sc, (slst, ch2, slst) into last ch to pass to other side of foundation chain, 1 sc, 1 hdc, 1 sc, slst to join.
Fasten off, leaving sufficient yarn for sewing to body (49).
Sew one ear to each side of the body between Rounds 4 and 5 (50).

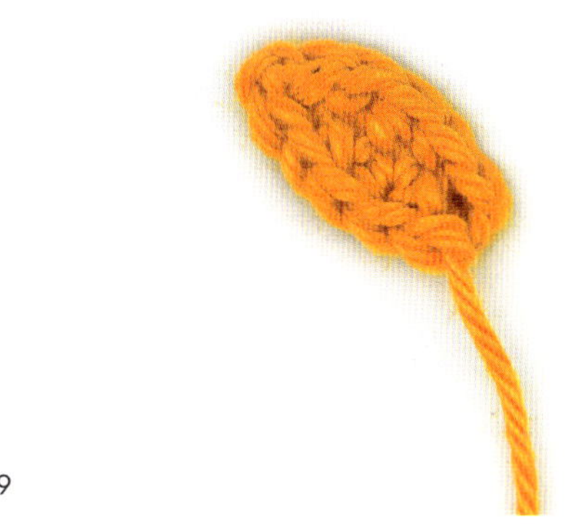

49

50

Spots (make 10)

Using Soil, make MR.
Round 1: 4 sc into MR, slst on RS to join. (4 sts)
Fasten off and weave in ends.
Stick the spots to the body *(51)*.
Add some blush under the eyes *(51)*.

51

MEDIUM-SIZED COMPANION

Body

Using Mustard, work the body according to instructions for the medium-sized body in Standard Parts: The Little Companions.

Horns (make 2)

Note: work in spiral rounds.

Using Soil.
Work as for the big companion's horns.
Sew the horns to the top of the body between Rounds 1 and 3.

Ears (make 2)

Note: work the ears in ovals around a foundation chain.

Using Mustard.
Work as for the big companion's ears.
Sew one ear to each side of the body between Rounds 4 and 5.

Spots (make 7)

Using Soil.
Work as for the big companion's spots.
Stick the spots to the body *(52)*.
Add some blush under the eyes *(52)*.

52

53

SMALL COMPANION

Body

Using Mustard, work the body according to instructions for the small body in Standard Parts: The Little Companions.

Horns (make 2)

Note: work in spiral rounds.

Using Soil, make MR.
Round 1: 4 sc into MR. (4 sts)
Round 2: 1 sc in each st around.
Change to Mustard.
Round 3: 1 sc in each st around.
Fasten off and cut, leaving enough yarn for sewing to body.
Sew the horns on top of the body between Rounds 1 and 3.

Ears (make 2)

Note: work the ears in ovals around a foundation chain.

Using Mustard, ch 5 and start in second ch from hook.
Round 1: slst, 2 sc, (slst, ch2, slst) into last ch to pass to other side of foundation chain, 2 sc, slst to join.
Fasten off, leaving sufficient yarn for sewing together.
Sew one ear to each side of the body between Rounds 4 and 5.

Spots (make 5)

Using Soil.
Repeat all the steps for the big Companion's spots.
Stick the spots to the body *(53)*.
Add some blush under the eyes *(53)*.

Yuki

Yuki is none other than Santa's right-hand girl! With the help of her little companions, she travels the world collecting gift lists from every good child.

Finished Size

Yuki: approx 9½in (24cm) tall
Companions: between 2in (5.5cm) and 3in (7.5cm) tall

Note :
Size may vary depending on your gauge (tension) and the yarn used

Tools and Materials

Yarn and Colors Must-Have yarn in the following colors:

Yarn and Colors Furry yarn in the following color:

White (n° 001 × 1)

US 4 (2.00mm) crochet hook
Fiberfill stuffing
2 x 7mm safety eyes
Basic tool kit
(see Materials)

Instructions

Note: always use X-shaped stitches and joined rounds, unless stated otherwise.

Legs (make 2)

Using Black, make MR.
Round 1: 6 sc into MR, slst to join. (6 sts)
Round 2: ch1, inc in each st around, slst to join. (12 sts)
Round 3: ch1, [1 sc, inc] 6 times, slst to join. (18 sts)
Rounds 4 and 5 (2 rounds): ch1, 1 sc in each st around, slst to join.
Round 6: ch1, 6 sc, dec 3 times, 6 sc, slst to join. (15 sts)
Round 7: ch1, 5 sc, dec, 1 sc, dec, 5 sc, slst to join. (13 sts)
Rounds 8–13 (6 rounds): ch1, 1 sc in each st around, slst to join.
Round 14: ch1, 2 sc, inc, 7 sc, inc, 2 sc, slst to join. (15 sts)
Rounds 15–17 (3 rounds): ch1, 1 sc in each st around, slst to join.
Round 18: ch1, 2 sc, dec, 7 sc, dec, 2 sc, slst to join. (13 sts)
Round 19: ch1, 2 sc, inc, 7 sc, inc, 2 sc, slst to join. (15 sts)
Stuff the foot.
Round 20: ch1, 3 sc, inc, 7 sc, inc, 3 sc, change to Limestone. (17 sts)
Round 21: slst BLO of each st around. (17 sts)
Round 22: 1 sc BLO of each st around, slst to join. (17 sts)
Round 23: ch1, 4 sc, inc, 7 sc, inc, 4 sc, slst to join. (19 sts)
Round 24: ch1, 1 sc in each st around, slst to join.
Round 25: ch1, 5 sc, inc, 7 sc, inc, 5 sc, slst to join. (21 sts)

Round 26: ch1, 1 sc in each st around, slst to join.
Round 27: ch1, 1 sc in each st around, change to Cardinal, slst to join.
Round 28: ch1, 1 sc in each st around, slst to join.
Round 29: ch1, 1 sc in each st, slst on RS to join.
Mark last slst.
Leg 1: fasten off and weave in ends.
Stuff leg firmly.
Leg 2: repeat steps as for leg 1, but at end, work last slst on WS. Stuff leg firmly. Do not mark last slst, do not cut yarn. Continue as follows:

Body

Note: see Diagram 2, Tecniques: joining the legs.

Round 30: ch1, 8 sc into leg 2, ch2, [1 sc into fourth st before marked slst, 3 sc, 1 sc into same st as marked slst, 16 sc] on leg 1, 2 sc into ch2, 13 sc into remaining sts of leg 2, slst to join. (46 sts)
Round 31: ch1, 8 sc into leg 2, 2 sc in opposite side of ch2, [dec, 21 sc] on leg 1, and [dec, 11 sc] on remaining sts of leg 2, slst to join. (44 sts)

Note: stuff as you go along.

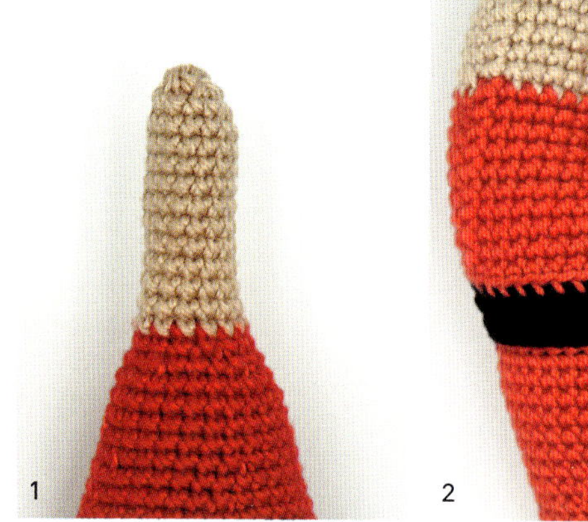

Rounds 32–35 (4 rounds): ch1, 1 sc in each st around, slst to join.
Round 36: ch1, 1 sc in each st around, work an additional 10 sc in order to start next round in middle of back, change to Black, slst BLO to join.
Round 37: ch1, 14 sc BLO, dec BLO, 10 sc BLO, dec BLO, 16 sc BLO, slst to join. (42 sts)
Round 38: ch1, 1 sc in each st around, slst to join.
Round 39: ch1, 13 sc, dec, 10 sc, dec, 15 sc, change to Cardinal. (40 sts)
Round 40: slst BLO of each st around.
Round 41: 1 sc BLO of each st around, slst to join.
Round 42: ch1, [8 sc, dec] 4 times, slst to join. (36 sts)
Rounds 43 and 44 (2 rounds): ch1, 1 sc in each st around, slst to join.
Round 45: ch1, [7 sc, dec] 4 times, slst to join. (32 sts)
Round 46: ch1, 1 sc in each st around, slst to join.
Round 47: ch1, [6 sc, dec] 4 times, slst to join. (28 sts)
Round 48: ch1, 1 sc in each st around, slst to join.
Round 49: ch1, [5 sc, dec] 4 times, slst to join. (24 sts)
Round 50: ch1, 1 sc in each st around, slst to join.
Round 51: ch1, 6 sc, dec, 10 sc, dec, 4 sc, slst to join. (22 sts)
Round 52: ch1, 1 sc in each st around, slst to join.
Round 53: ch1, 6 sc, dec, 10 sc, dec, 2 sc, slst to join. (20 sts)
Round 54: ch1, [3 sc, dec] 4 times, slst to join. (16 sts)
Round 55: ch1, [3 sc, dec] twice, 4 sc, dec, change to Limestone, slst to join. (13 sts)
Rounds 56–66 (11 rounds): ch1, 1 sc in each st around, slst to join.
Round 67: ch1, 5 sc, dec, 6 sc, slst to join. (12 sts)

Note: strengthen the neck (see Techniques: Strengthening the Neck).

Round 68: ch1, dec 6 times, slst to join. (6 sts)
Cut the yarn and fasten off (1).

Skirt

PART 1

Holding the body neck down, join Cardinal yarn to FLO of first st of Round 36 (2).
Round 1: ch2, [2 hdc, hdc-inc] 14 times, 2 hdc, slst to join. (58 sts)
Round 2: ch2, [7 hdc, hdc-inc] 7 times, 2 hdc, slst BLO to join. (65 sts)
Round 3: ch2, 1 hdc BLO of each st around, slst to join.
Round 4: ch2, [8 hdc, hdc-inc], 7 times, 2 hdc, slst to join. (72 sts)
Round 5: ch2, 1 hdc in each st, slst to join.
Round 6: ch2, [9 hdc, hdc-inc], 7 times, 2 hdc, slst to join. (79 sts)
Round 7: ch2, 1 hdc in each st, slst to join.
Round 8: ch2, [18 hdc, hdc-inc] 4 times, 3 hdc. (83 sts)
Round 9: slst in each st around.
Fasten off and weave in ends.

PART 2

Holding the body neck down, join Cardinal yarn to FLO of first st of Round 2 (3).
Round 1: [ch4, sk 1 st, slst] 41 times, slst to join.
Fasten off and weave in ends (4).
Glue the Furry White yarn all round the bottom of the skirt (5).

BELT BOW

Part 1

Note: work part 1 along a foundation chain.

Using Marble, ch10 and start in third ch from hook.
Row 1: 8 hdc, turn (8 sts)
Row 2: ch2, 8 hdc.
Row 3: 3 slst on first side of rectangle, 8 slst on second, 3 slst on third, 8 slst on fourth (6).
Fasten off and weave in ends (7).

Part 2

Note: work part 2 along a foundation chain.

Using Cardinal, ch9 and start in third ch from hook.
Row 1: 7 hdc. (7 sts)
Row 2: 2 slst on first side of rectangle, 7 slst on second, 2 slst on third, 7 slst on fourth (6).
Fasten off and weave in ends (7).

3

4

5

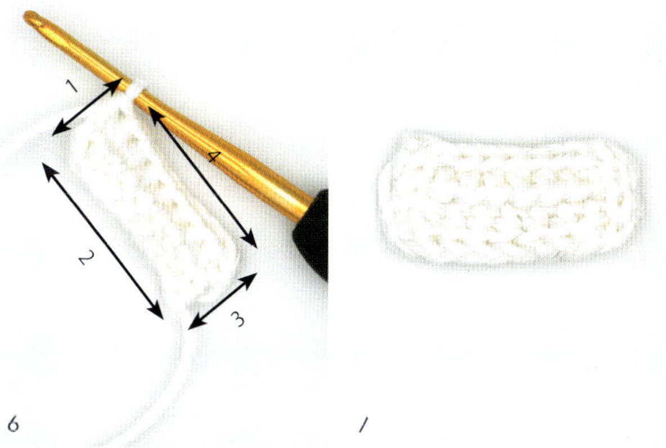

6

7

Lay the red rectangle on the white rectangle.
Wrap some Cardinal yarn several times round the 2 rectangles and knot.
Sew the bow on to the middle of the belt (8).

Arms (make 2)

Using Black, make MR.
Round 1: 6 sc into MR, slst to join. (6 sts)
Round 2: ch1, [1 sc, inc] 3 times, slst to join. (9 sts)
Round 3: ch1, [2 sc, inc] 3 times, slst to join. (12 sts)
Round 4: ch1, 1 sc in each st around, slst to join.
Round 5: ch1, 5 sc, dec, 5 sc, slst to join. (11 sts)
Round 6: ch1, 5 sc, 1 3sc-bo (= thumb), 5 sc, slst to join.
Round 7: ch1, 5 sc, dec, 2 sc, dec, slst to join. (9 sts)
Round 8: ch1, 1 sc in each st around, slst to join.
Round 9: ch1, 5 sc, dec, 2 sc, change to Cardinal, slst to join. (8 sts)
Stuff hand firmly.
Rounds 10–18 (9 rounds): ch1, 1 sc in each st around, slst to join.
Round 19: ch1, 4 sc, dec, 2 sc, slst to join. (7 sts)
Rounds 20–24 (5 rounds): ch1, 1 sc in each st around, slst to join.
Stuff the arms lightly halfway.
Flatten out the opening then work 3 sc through both thicknesses at the same time to close.
Fasten off and cut, leaving enough yarn for sewing to body.
Stick the Furry White yarn around the wrist at the color change (9).

Sew one arm to each side of the body between Rounds 54 and 55, ensuring that the thumbs are positioned at the front (10).

Head

Using Limestone, make MR.
Round 1: 6 sc into MR, slst to join. (6 sts)
Round 2: ch1, inc in each st around, slst to join. (12 sts)
Round 3: ch1, [1 sc, inc] 6 times, slst to join. (18 sts)
Round 4: ch1, [1 sc, inc, 1 sc] 6 times, slst to join. (24 sts)
Round 5: ch1, [3 sc, inc] 6 times, slst to join. (30 sts)
Round 6: ch1, [2 sc, inc, 2 sc] 6 times, slst to join. (36 sts)
Round 7: ch1, [5 sc, inc] 6 times, slst to join. (42 sts)
Round 8: ch1, [3 sc, inc, 3 sc] 6 times, slst to join. (48 sts)
Round 9: ch1, [7 sc, inc] 6 times, slst to join. (54 sts)

8 9 10

11

12 13

Round 10: ch1, [4 sc, inc, 4 sc] 6 times, slst to join. (60 sts)
Round 11: ch1, 1 sc in each st around, slst to join.
Round 12: ch1, [9 sc, inc] 6 times, slst to join. (66 sts)
Round 13: ch1, 1 sc in each st around, slst to join.
Round 14: ch1, 16 sc, inc, 32 sc, inc, 16 sc, slst to join. (68 sts)
Rounds 15–23 (9 rounds): ch1, 1 sc in each st around, slst to join. (68 sts)
Round 24: ch1, 28 sc, ch1, sk 1 st, 10 sc, ch1, sk 1 st, 28 sc, slst to join.
Round 25: ch1, 28 sc, 1 sc into ch, 10 sc, 1 sc into ch, 28 sc, slst to join.
Round 26: ch1, 16 sc, dec, 32 sc, dec, 16 sc, slst to join. (66 sts)
Round 27: ch1, 1 sc in each st around, slst to join.
Round 28: ch1, 15 sc, dec, 32 sc, dec, 15 sc, slst to join. (64 sts)
Insert the eyes into the holes formed by the skipped sts in Round 24.
Round 29: ch1, [14 sc, dec] 4 times, slst to join. (60 sts)
Round 30: ch1, [4 sc, dec, 4 sc] 6 times, slst to join. (54 sts)
Round 31: ch1, [7 sc, dec] 6 times, slst to join. (48 sts)
Round 32: ch1, [4 sc, dec] 8 times, slst to join. (40 sts)
Round 33: ch1, [3 sc, dec] 8 times, slst to join. (32 sts)
Start to stuff.
Round 34: ch1, [2 sc, dec] 8 times, slst to join. (24 sts)
Round 35: ch1, [1 sc, dec] 8 times, slst BLO to join. (16 sts)
Round 36: ch1, 1 sc BLO of each st around, slst to join.
Rounds 37–41 (5 rounds): ch1, 1 sc in each st around, slst to join.
Fasten off and weave in ends. Complete the stuffing.
Push Rounds 36–41 inside the head (11).
Using White floss, embroider the whites of the eyes, then add a touch of Purple floss to the sides of the eyes (12).
Using Black floss, embroider the black above the eyes and finish by embroidering the eye lashes (13).
Using Brown floss, embroider the eyebrows between Rounds 20 and 22 (14).
Using Limestone, embroider the nose between Rounds 26 and 27. Use a brush and some blush to add a little color to the cheeks and above the nose (15).

Note: the circumference of the head once stuffed is approximately 7½in (19 cm).

EARS (MAKE 2)

Using Limestone, make MR.
Round 1: 1 sc, 4 hdc, 1 sc into MR. (6 sts)
Fasten off, leaving sufficient yarn for sewing to head.
Sew one ear to each side of the head between Rounds 23 and 27, leaving a gap of 8 sts between ear and eye (16, 17).

ATTACH THE HEAD

Using Limestone, attach the head according to instructions in Techniques: Attaching the Head. Leave 3 rounds in Limestone visible.

14 15 16 17 18

COLLAR

Stick the Furry White yarn around the neck at the color change (18).

Hair

PART 1

Using Grape, make MR.
Round 1: 6 sc into MR, slst to join. (6 sts)
Round 2: ch1, inc in each st around, slst FLO to join. (12 sts)
Round 3: ch1, [1 sc FLO, inc FLO] 6 times, slst FLO to join. (18 sts)
Round 4: ch1, [1 sc FLO, inc FLO, 1 sc FLO] 6 times, slst to join. (24 sts)
Round 5: ch1, [3 sc, inc] 6 times, slst to join. (30 sts)
Do not cut the yarn and continue with the strands of hair.

Note: it is the WS of the strands of hair that will be visible.

Strands 1 and 2 (2 strands): ch27, and starting in second ch from hook: slst, 25 sc, slst into next st of Round 5 to join.
Strands 3–10 (8 strands): ch16, and starting in second ch from hook: 15 sc, slst into next st of Round 5 to join.
Strands 11 and 12 (2 strands): repeat strands 1 and 2.
Strands 13–30 (18 strands): ch30, and starting in second ch from hook: 29 sc, slst into next st of Round 5 to join.
Fasten off and weave in ends *(19)*.

PART 2

Join Grape yarn to BLO of first st of Round 3 of Part 1 *(20)*.
Strand 1: ch27, and starting in second ch from hook: slst, 25 sc, slst BLO of next st of Round 3 to join.
Strands 2–5 (4 strands): ch18, and starting in second ch from hook: 17 sc, slst BLO of next st of Round 3 to join.
Strand 6: repeat strand 1.
Strands 7–18 (12 strands): ch32, and starting in second ch from hook: 31 sc, slst BLO of next st of Round 3 to join.
Fasten off and weave in ends *(21)*.

PART 3

Join Grape yarn to BLO of first st of Round 2 of Part 1 *(22)*.
Strands 1–3 (3 strands): ch19, and starting in second ch from hook: 18 sc, slst BLO of next st of Round 2 to join.
Strands 4–12 (9 strands): ch33, and starting in second ch from hook: 32 sc, slst BLO of next st of Round 2 to join.
Fasten off and weave in ends *(23)*.

PART 4 (MAKE 2)

Using Grape, make MR.
Round 1: ch2, 8 dc into MR, slst to join. (8 sts)
Do not cut the yarn. Continue with the strands of hair.

Note: it is the WS of the strands of hair that will be visible.

Strands 1–8 (8 strands): ch20, and starting in second ch from hook: slst, 18 sc, slst into next st of Round 1.
Fasten off, leaving sufficient yarn for sewing to head *(24)*.

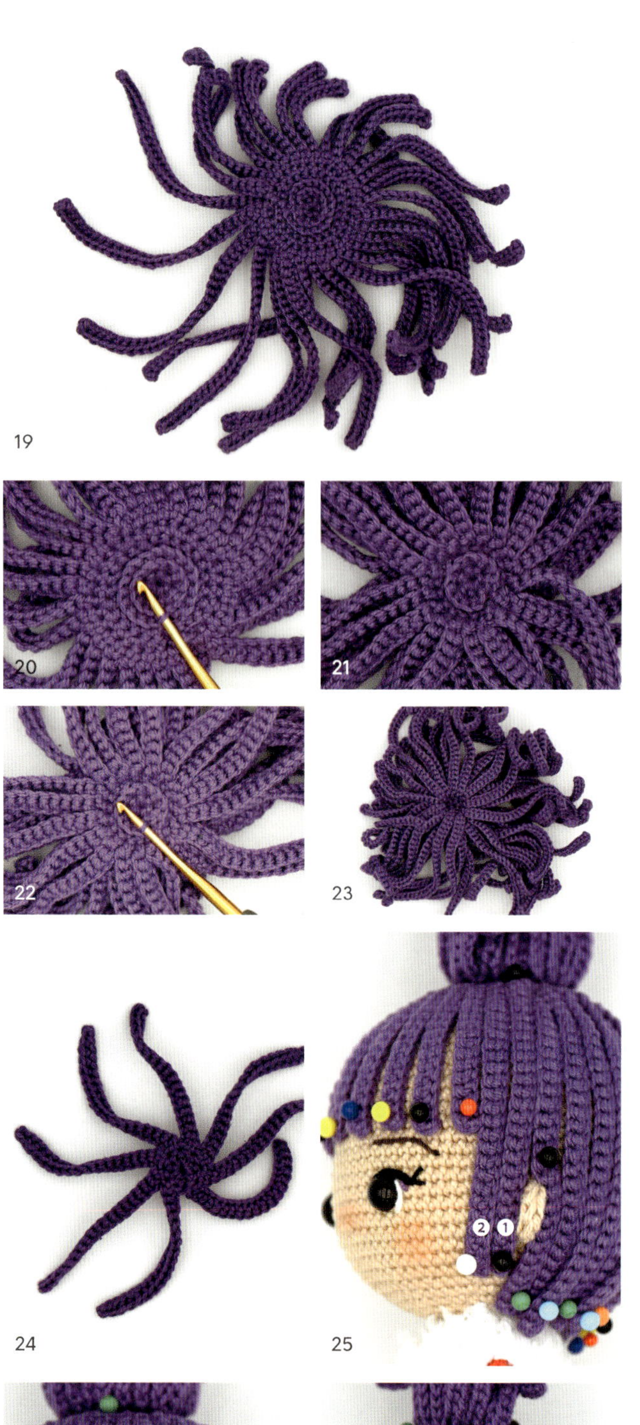

19 20 21 22 23 24 25

26

27

ATTACH THE HAIR

Arrange the hair on the head, starting by placing the center of the MR of the hair on the center of the MR of the head. Hold in place with a pin.

Holding Parts 2 and 3 together on top of the head with hair elastic will make things easier.

Part 1: position strands 1, 2, 11, and 12 in front of the ears (25, 26).

Stick down the strands one by one, applying glue to each strand. Hold in place with pins until the glue has dried.

Glue strands 3–10 to the forehead (27).

Glue all the remaining strands around the head (28). It does not matter if there are a few little gaps between the strands – they will be filled in later.

Part 2: glue strands 1 and 6 in front of the ears (29, 30).

Glue strands 2–5 to the forehead (31).

Glue the remaining strands around the head (32).

Part 3: stick strands 1–3 on the forehead (33).

Glue the remaining strands around the head (34).

Part 4: glue or sew the MRs to each side of the head (35, 36).

Hat

Using Cardinal, make MR.

Round 1: 6 sc into MR, slst to join. (6 sts)
Round 2: ch1, 1 sc in each st around, slst to join. (6 sts)
Round 3: ch1, [1 sc, inc] 3 times, slst to join. (9 sts)
Round 4: ch1, 1 sc in each st around, slst to join.
Round 5: ch1, [2 sc, inc] 3 times, slst to join. (12 sts)
Round 6: ch1, 1 sc in each st around, slst to join.
Round 7: ch1, [3 sc, inc] 3 times, slst to join. (15 sts)
Round 8: ch1, 1 sc in each st around, slst to join.
Round 9: ch1, [4 sc, inc] 3 times, slst to join. (18 sts)
Round 10: ch1, 1 sc in each st around, slst to join.
Round 11: ch1, [5 sc, inc] 3 times, slst to join. (21 sts)
Round 12: ch1, 1 sc in each st around, slst to join.
Round 13: ch1, [6 sc, inc] 3 times, slst to join. (24 sts)
Round 14: ch1, 1 sc in each st around, slst to join.
Round 15: ch1, [7 sc, inc] 3 times, slst to join. (27 sts)
Round 16: ch1, 1 sc in each st around, slst to join.
Round 17: ch1, [8 sc, inc] 3 times, slst to join. (30 sts)
Round 18: ch1, 1 sc in each st around, slst to join.
Round 19: ch1, [9 sc, inc] 3 times, slst to join. (33 sts)
Round 20: ch1, 1 sc in each st around, slst to join.
Round 21: ch1, [10 sc, inc] 3 times, slst to join. (36 sts)
Round 22: ch1, 1 sc in each st around, slst to join.
Round 23: ch1, [11 sc, inc] 3 times, slst to join. (39 sts)
Round 24: ch1, 1 sc in each st around, slst to join.
Round 25: ch1, [12 sc, inc] 3 times, slst to join. (42 sts)
Round 26: ch1, 1 sc in each st around, slst to join.

Round 27: ch1, [6 sc, inc] 6 times, slst to join. (48 sts)
Round 28: ch1, 1 sc in each st around, slst to join.
Round 29: ch1, [7 sc, inc] 6 times, slst to join. (54 sts)
Round 30: ch1, 1 sc in each st around, slst to join.
Round 31: ch1, [8 sc, inc] 6 times, slst to join. (60 sts)
Round 32: ch1, [9 sc, inc] 6 times, slst to join. (66 sts)
Round 33: ch1, [10 sc, inc] 6 times. (72 sts)
Round 34: slst in each st around.

Fasten off and weave in ends *(37)*.
Glue the Furry White yarn around the base of the hat *(38)*.
Using Furry White, make a pompom 1½in (4cm) in diameter, and sew to top of hat *(39)*.
Fold top of hat and hold in place by sticking side of pompom to side of hat *(40)*.
Stick hat to side of head *(41)*.

37 38

39 40

41

Shoes (make 2)

SOLES

Using Black, make the soles according to instructions in Standard Parts: Soles of the Shoes.

42 43

MAIN BODY OF SHOE

Join Black yarn to BLO of third slst of previous round (42).
Round 1: 1 sc BLO of each st around, slst to join. (25 sts)
Rounds 2 and 3 (2 rounds): ch1, 1 sc in each st around, slst to join.
Round 4: ch1, 7 sc [1 sc, dec] 4 times, 6 sc, slst to join. (21 sts)
Round 5: ch1, 8 sc, dec, 3 sc, dec, 6 sc, slst to join. (19 sts)
Rounds 6–9 (4 rounds): ch1, 1 sc in each st around, slst to join.
Round 10: ch1, 1 sc in each st around, slst on RS to join.
Fasten off and weave in ends (43).

44

FLOWERS FOR SHOES (MAKE 2)

Note: work the flower along a foundation chain.

Using Pepper, ch5 and start in fifth ch from hook.
Row 1: slst, [ch5, slst into fifth ch from hook] 5 times (44).
Roll the chain up to make the flower and sew all the layers together.
Fasten off and weave in ends.
Stick the flower to the shoe (45).

45

The Little Companions

BIG COMPANION

Body

Using Marble, work the body according to instructions for the big body in Standard Parts: The Little Companions.

Hat

Using Cardinal, make MR.
Round 1: 6 sc into MR, slst to join. (6 sts)
Round 2: ch1, 1 sc in each st around, slst to join.
Round 3: ch1, [1 sc, inc] 3 times, slst to join. (9 sts)
Round 4: ch1, 1 sc in each st around, slst to join.
Round 5: ch1, [2 sc, inc] 3 times, slst to join. (12 sts)
Round 6: ch1, [3 sc, inc] 3 times, slst to join. (15 sts)
Round 7: ch1, [4 sc, inc] 3 times, slst to join. (18 sts)
Round 8: ch1, 1 sc in each st around, slst to join.
Round 9: ch1, [5 sc, inc] 3 times. (21 sts)
Round 10: slst in each st around.
Fasten off and weave in ends.
Stick Furry White yarn to the top and around base of the hat.
Stick the hat to the side of the head (46).

46

Scarf

Note: work the scarf along a foundation chain.

Using Cardinal, ch66 and start in third ch from hook.
Row 1: 64 dc. (64 sts)
Fasten off and weave in ends.
Glue Furry White yarn to each end of the scarf.
Add some blush under the eyes.
Sew the scarf around the body (47).

47

MEDIUM-SIZED COMPANION

Body

Using Marble work the body according to instructions for the medium-sized body in Standard Parts: The Little Companions.

Hat

Using Cardinal, make MR.
Round 1: 6 sc into MR, slst to join. (6 sts)
Round 2: ch1, 1 sc in each st around, slst to join.
Round 3: ch1, [1 sc, inc] 3 times, slst to join. (9 sts)
Round 4: ch1, 1 sc in each st around, slst to join.
Round 5: ch1, [2 sc, inc] 3 times, slst to join. (12 sts)
Round 6: ch1, [3 sc, inc] 3 times, slst to join. (15 sts)
Round 7: ch1, 1 sc in each st around, slst to join.
Round 8: ch1, [4 sc, inc] 3 times. (18 sts)
Round 9: slst in each st around.
Fasten off and weave in ends.
Stick Furry White yarn to the top and around the base of the hat.
Stick the hat to the side of the head.

Scarf

Note: work the scarf along a foundation chain.

Using Cardinal, ch52 and start in third ch from hook.
Row 1: 50 dc. (50 sts)
Fasten off and weave in ends.
Glue Furry White yarn to each end of the scarf.
Add some blush under the eyes.
Sew the scarf around the body (48).

48

49

SMALL COMPANION

Body

Using Marble, work the body according to instructions for the small body in Standard Parts: The Little Companions.

Hat

Using Cardinal, make MR.
Round 1: 6 sc into MR, slst to join. (6 sts)
Round 2: ch1, 1 sc in each st around, slst to join.
Round 3: ch1, [1 sc, inc] 3 times, slst to join. (9 sts)
Round 4: ch1, 1 sc in each st around, slst to join.
Round 5: ch1, [2 sc, inc] 3 times, slst to join. (12 sts)
Round 6: ch1, 1 sc in each st around, slst to join.
Round 7: ch1, [3 sc, inc] 3 times. (15 sts)
Round 8: slst in each st around.
Fasten off and weave in ends.
Stick Furry White yarn to the top and around base of hat.
Stick hat to side of the head.

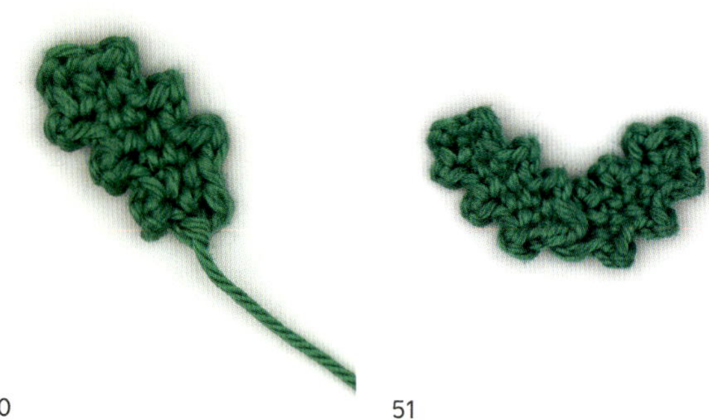

50 51

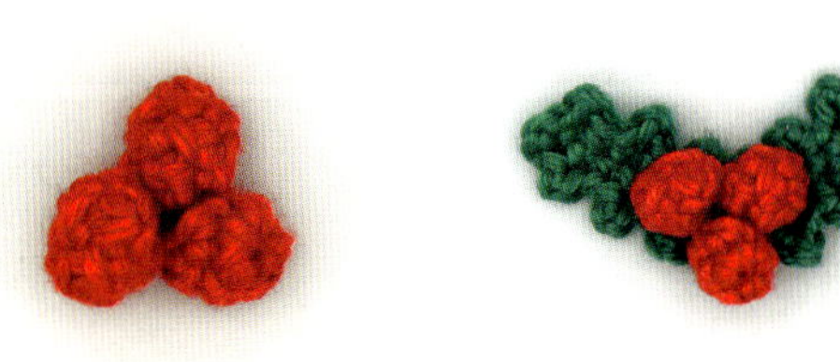

52 53

Scarf

Note: work the scarf along a foundation chain.

Using Cardinal, ch47 and start in third ch from hook.
Row 1: 45 hdc. (45 sts)
Fasten off and weave in ends.
Glue Furry White yarn to each end of the scarf.
Add some blush under the eyes.
Sew the scarf around the body (49).

The Holly

LEAVES (MAKE 2)

Note: work the leaves in ovals around a foundation chain.

Using Green Beryl, ch9 and start in second ch from hook.
Round 1: slst, 1 sc, [ch2, slst into second ch from hook, 2 sc into foundation chain] 3 times, ch1 to pass to other side of foundation chain, 1 sc, [ch2, slst into second ch from hook, 2 sc into foundation chain] twice, ch2, slst into second ch from hook, 1 sc into foundation chain, slst to join.
Fasten off, leaving sufficient yarn for sewing together (50).
Form a "V" shape, overlapping the bases of the 2 leaves, and sew together (51).

BERRIES (MAKE 3)

Note: work in spiral rounds.

Using Pepper, make MR.
Round 1: 4 sc into MR. (4 sts)
Round 2: [1 sc, inc] twice. (6 sts)
Round 3: [1 sc, dec] twice. (4 sts)
Fasten off and weave in ends.
Stick the 3 berries together (52), then stick them onto the leaves (53).

Kitsune

Kitsune loves foxes and their pretty colors so much that she made herself a costume so that she could live with them in the woods. She loves this new life surrounded by her little friends!

Finished Size

Kitsune: approx 8½in (21.5cm) tall
Companions: between 1½in (4cm) and 2¼in (6cm) tall

Note :
Size may vary depending on your gauge (tension) and the yarn used

Tools and Materials

Yarn and Colors Must-Have yarn in the following colors:

Cream (n° 002 × 1)
Sorbus (n° 019 × 1)
Black (n° 100 × 1)
Ecru (n° 003 × 1)
Green Beryl (n° 077 × 1)

US 4 (2.00mm) crochet hook
Fiberfill stuffing
2 x 7mm safety eyes
Basic tool kit
(see Materials)

Instructions

Note: always use X-shaped stitches and joined rounds, unless stated otherwise.

Legs (make 2)

Using Cream, make MR.
Round 1: 6 sc into MR, slst to join. (6 sts)
Round 2: ch1, inc in each st around, slst to join. (12 sts)
Round 3: ch1, [1 sc, inc] 6 times, slst to join. (18 sts)
Rounds 4 and 5 (2 rounds): ch1, 1 sc in each st around, slst to join.
Round 6: ch1, 6 sc, dec 3 times, 6 sc, slst to join. (15 sts)
Round 7: ch1, 5 sc, dec, 1 sc, dec, 5 sc, slst to join. (13 sts)
Rounds 8–11 (4 rounds): ch1, 1 sc in each st around, slst to join.
Round 12: ch1, 1 sc in each st around, change to Sorbus, slst to join.
Round 13: ch1, 1 sc in each st, slst to join.
Round 14: ch1, 2 sc, inc, 7 sc, inc, 2 sc, slst to join. (15 sts)
Rounds 15–17 (3 rounds): ch1, 1 sc in each st around, slst to join.
Round 18: ch1, 2 sc, dec, 7 sc, dec, 2 sc, slst to join. (13 sts)
Round 19: ch1, 2 sc, inc, 7 sc, inc, 2 sc, slst to join. (15 sts)
Stuff the foot.
Round 20: ch1, 3 sc, inc, 7 sc, inc, 3 sc, slst to join. (17 sts)
Round 21: ch1, 1 sc in each st around, slst to join.
Round 22: ch1, 4 sc, inc, 7 sc, inc, 4 sc, slst to join. (19 sts)
Round 23: ch1, 1 sc in each st around, slst to join.

Round 24: ch1, 5 sc, inc, 7 sc, inc, 5 sc, slst to join. (21 sts)
Rounds 25–27 (3 rounds): ch1, 1 sc in each st around, slst to join.
Round 28: ch1, 1 sc in each st around, slst on RS to join.
Mark last slst.
Leg 1: fasten off and weave in ends.
Stuff leg firmly, then continue as follows:

CUFF OF SOCK (MAKE 2)

Note: work cuff of sock along a foundation chain.

Using Cream, ch5 and start in second ch from hook.
Row 1: 4 sc, ch1, turn. (4 sts)
Row 2: 4 sc BLO, ch1, turn.
Repeat Row 2 until the cuff of the sock is long enough to go round the leg over the color change.
Fasten off, leaving sufficient yarn for sewing to leg *(1)*.
Sew around the leg, between Rounds 10 and 23 *(2)*.
Leg 2: repeat the steps as for leg 1, but at end, work last slst on WS.
Stuff leg firmly. Do not mark last slst, do not cut yarn.
Attach a cuff as for leg 1 and continue as follows:

Body

Note: see Diagram 2, Techniques: Joining the Legs.

Round 29: ch1, 8 sc into leg 2, ch2, [1 sc into fourth st before marked slst, 3 sc, 1 sc into same st as marked slst, 16 sc] on leg 1, 2 sc into ch2 and 13 sc into remaining sts of leg 2, slst to join. (46 sts)

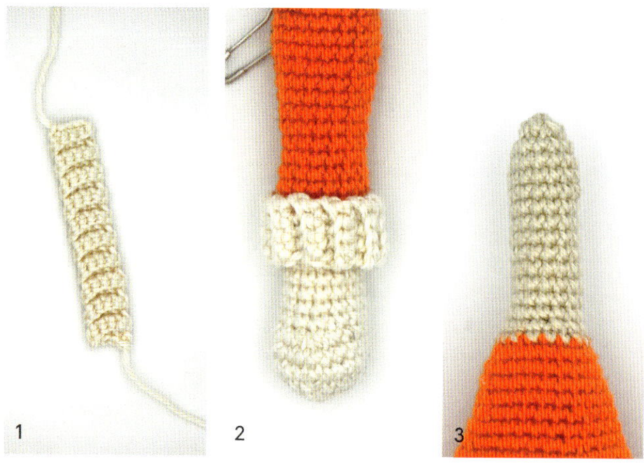

Round 30: ch1, 8 sc into leg 2, 2 sc in opposite side of ch2, [dec, 21 sc] on leg 1, and [dec, 11 sc] on remaining sts of leg 2, slst to join. (44 sts)

Note: stuff as you go along.

Rounds 31–34 (4 rounds): ch1, 1 sc in each st around, slst to join.
Round 35: ch1, 1 sc in each st around, work an additional 10 sc in order to start next round in middle of back, slst to join.
Round 36: ch1, 14 sc, dec, 11 sc, dec, 15 sc, slst to join. (42 sts)
Round 37: ch1, 1 sc in each st around, slst to join.
Round 38: ch1, 13 sc, dec, 11 sc, dec, 14 sc, slst to join. (40 sts)
Round 39: ch1, 1 sc in each st around, slst to join.
Round 40: ch1, [8 sc, dec] 4 times, slst to join. (36 sts)
Rounds 41 and 42 (2 rounds): ch1, 1 sc in each st around, slst to join.
Round 43: ch1, [7 sc, dec] 4 times, slst to join. (32 sts)
Round 44: ch1, 1 sc in each st around, slst to join.
Round 45: ch1, [6 sc, dec] 4 times, slst to join. (28 sts)
Round 46: ch1, 1 sc in each st around, slst to join.
Round 47: ch1, [5 sc, dec] 4 times, slst to join. (24 sts)
Round 48: ch1, 1 sc in each st around, slst to join.
Round 49: ch1, 6 sc, dec, 10 sc, dec, 4 sc, slst to join. (22 sts)
Round 50: ch1, 1 sc in each st around, slst to join.
Round 51: ch1, 5 sc, dec, 9 sc, dec, 4 sc, change to Ecru, slst to join. (20 sts)
Round 52: ch1, [3 sc, dec] 4 times, slst to join. (16 sts)
Round 53: ch1, [3 sc, dec] twice, 4 sc, dec, slst to join. (13 sts)
Rounds 54–64 (11 rounds): ch1, 1 sc in each st around, slst to join.
Round 65: ch1, 5 sc, dec, 6 sc, slst to join. (12 sts)

Note: strengthen the neck (see Techniques: Strengthening the Neck).

Round 66: ch1, dec 6 times, slst to join. (6 sts)
Cut the yarn and fasten off *(3)*.

BORDER OF SWEATER

Note: work the border of the sweater along a foundation chain.

Using Cream, ch5 and start in third ch from hook.
Row 1: 3 hdc, ch2, turn. (3 sts)
Row 2: 3 hdc BLO, ch2, turn.
Repeat Row 2 until the strip is long enough to go round the body at Round 38.
Fasten off and cut, leaving enough yarn for sewing to the body.
Sew around the body, between Rounds 36 and 40 *(4)*.
Using Cream, embroider little "Vs" on the sweater *(5)*.

4 5

Arms (make 2)

Using Ecru, make MR.
Round 1: 6 sc into MR, slst to join. (6 sts)
Round 2: ch1, [1 sc, inc] 3 times, slst to join. (9 sts)
Round 3: ch1, [2 sc, inc] 3 times, slst to join. (12 sts)
Round 4: ch1, 1 sc in each st around, slst to join.
Round 5: ch1, 5 sc, dec, 5 sc, slst to join. (11 sts)
Round 6: ch1, 5 sc, 1 3sc-bo (= thumb), 5 sc, slst to join.
Round 7: ch1, 5 sc, dec, 2 sc, dec, slst to join. (9 sts)
Round 8: ch1, 1 sc in each st around, change to Sorbus, slst to join.
Round 9: ch1, 5 sc, dec, 2 sc, slst to join. (8 sts)
Stuff hand firmly.
Rounds 10–18 (9 rounds): ch1, 1 sc in each st around, slst to join.
Round 19: ch1, 4 sc, dec, 2 sc, slst to join. (7 sts)
Rounds 20–23 (4 rounds): ch1, 1 sc in each st around, slst to join.
Round 24: ch1, 1 sc in each st, slst on RS to join.
Stuff the arms lightly halfway.
Flatten out the opening then work 3 sc through both thicknesses at the same time to close.
Fasten off and cut, leaving enough yarn for sewing to body.

6

7

8

CUFFS OF SLEEVES (MAKE 2)

Note: work the cuffs of the sleeves along a foundation chain.

Using Cream, ch5 and start in third ch from hook.
Row 1: 3 hdc, ch2, turn. (3 sts)
Row 2: 3 hdc BLO, ch2, turn.
Repeat Row 2 until the cuff is long enough to go round the arm at Round 9.
Fasten off and cut, leaving enough yarn for sewing to arms.
Sew around the arm, between Rounds 7 and 10 *(6)*.
Sew one arm to each side of the body at the color change, ensuring that the thumbs are positioned at the front *(7, 8)*.

Head

Using Ecru, make MR.
Round 1: 6 sc into MR, slst to join. (6 sts)
Round 2: ch1, inc in each st around, slst to join. (12 sts)
Round 3: ch1, [1 sc, inc] 6 times, slst to join. (18 sts)
Round 4: ch1, [1 sc, inc, 1 sc] 6 times, slst to join. (24 sts)
Round 5: ch1, [3 sc, inc] 6 times, slst to join. (30 sts)
Round 6: ch1, [2 sc, inc, 2 sc] 6 times, slst to join. (36 sts)
Round 7: ch1, [5 sc, inc] 6 times, slst to join. (42 sts)
Round 8: ch1, [3 sc, inc, 3 sc] 6 times, slst to join. (48 sts)
Round 9: ch1, [7 sc, inc] 6 times, slst to join. (54 sts)
Round 10: ch1, [4 sc, inc, 4 sc] 6 times, slst to join. (60 sts)
Round 11: ch1, 1 sc in each st around, slst to join.
Round 12: ch1, [9 sc, inc] 6 times, slst to join. (66 sts)
Round 13: ch1, 1 sc in each st around, slst to join.
Round 14: ch1, 16 sc, inc, 32 sc, inc, 16 sc, slst to join. (68 sts)
Rounds 15–23 (9 rounds): ch1, 1 sc in each st around, slst to join.
Round 24: ch1, 28 sc, ch1, sk 1 st, 10 sc, ch1, sk 1 st, 28 sc, slst to join.
Round 25: ch1, 28 sc, 1 sc into ch, 10 sc, 1 sc into ch, 28 sc, slst to join.
Round 26: ch1, 16 sc, dec, 32 sc, dec, 16 sc, slst to join. (66 sts)
Round 27: ch1, 1 sc in each st around, slst to join.
Round 28: ch1, 15 sc, dec, 32 sc, dec, 15 sc, slst to join. (64 sts)
Insert the eyes into the holes formed by the skipped sts in Round 24.
Round 29: ch1, [14 sc, dec] 4 times, slst to join. (60 sts)

Round 30: ch1, [4 sc, dec, 4 sc] 6 times, slst to join. (54 sts)
Round 31: ch1, [7 sc, dec] 6 times, slst to join. (48 sts)
Round 32: ch1, [4 sc, dec] 8 times, slst to join. (40 sts)
Round 33: ch1, [3 sc, dec] 8 times, slst to join. (32 sts)
Start to stuff.
Round 34: ch1, [2 sc, dec] 8 times, slst to join. (24 sts)
Round 35: ch1, [1 sc, dec] 8 times, slst BLO to join. (16 sts)
Round 36: ch1, 1 sc BLO of each st around, slst to join.
Rounds 37–41 (5 rounds): ch1, 1 sc in each st around, slst to join.
Fasten off and weave in ends. Complete the stuffing.
Push Rounds 36–41 inside the head *(9)*.
Using White floss, embroider the whites of the eyes *(10)*, then add a touch of Brown floss to the sides of the eyes *(11)*.
Using Black floss, embroider the black above the eyes and finish by embroidering the eyelashes *(12)*.
Using Brown floss, embroider the eyebrows between Rounds 20 and 22 *(13)*.
Using Ecru, embroider the nose between Rounds 26 and 27.
Use a brush and some blush to add a little color to the cheeks and above the nose *(14)*.

Note: the circumference of the head once stuffed is approximately 7½in (19cm).

9

10

11

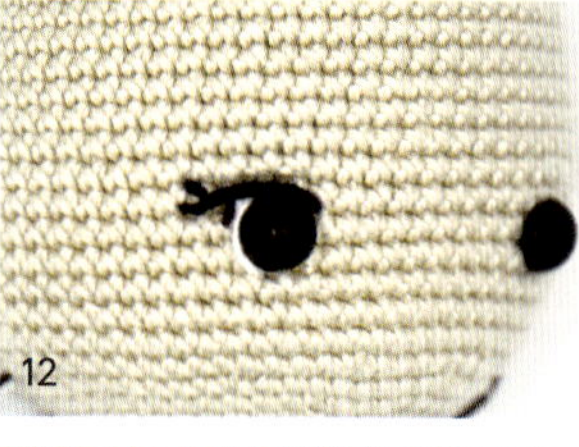
12

13

14

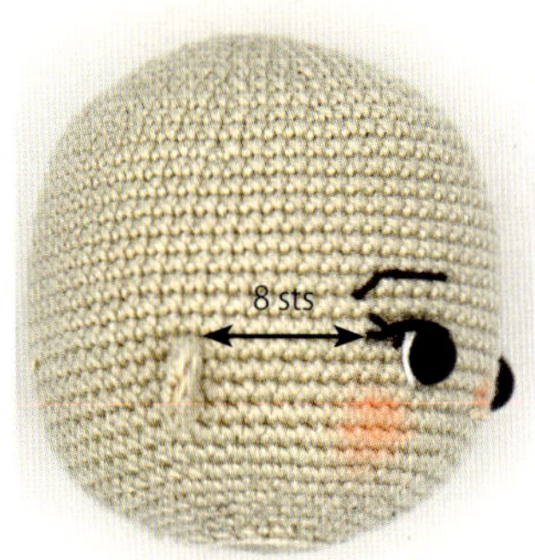

15

16

17

18

EARS (MAKE 2)

Using Ecru, make MR.
Round 1: 1 sc, 4 hdc, 1 sc into MR. (6 sts)
Fasten off, leaving sufficient yarn for sewing to head.
Sew one ear to each side of the head between Rounds 23 and 27, leaving a gap of 8 sts between ear and eye *(15, 16)*.

ATTACH THE HEAD

Using Ecru, attach the head according to instructions in Techniques: Attaching the Head. Leave 4 rounds in Ecru visible.

Scarf

Note: work the scarf along a foundation chain.

Using Cream, ch8 and start in third ch from hook.
Row 1: 6 dc, ch2, turn. (6 sts)
Row 2: 6 dc BLO, ch2, turn.
Repeat Row 2 until the scarf is long enough to go round the neck.
Make sure the scarf is a little loose.
Work 2 additional rows so you can cross the ends over.
At the end of the last row, work ch1, not 2, and turn.
Row 3: 6 slst BLO.
Fasten off and cut, leaving enough yarn for sewing to the neck.
Sew around the neck so that the last round of slst overlaps the other end of the scarf *(17)*.
Using Black, embroider 2 French knots at the point where the ends of the scarf overlap *(18)*.

Hair

PART 1

Using Black, make MR.
Round 1: 6 sc into MR, slst to join. (6 sts)
Round 2: ch1, inc in each st around, slst FLO to join. (12 sts)
Round 3: ch1, [1 sc FLO, inc FLO] 6 times, slst FLO to join. (18 sts)
Round 4: ch1, [1 sc FLO, inc FLO, 1 sc FLO] 6 times, slst to join. (24 sts)
Round 5: ch1, [3 sc, inc] 6 times, slst to join. (30 sts)
Do not cut the yarn and continue with the strands of hair.

Note: it is the WS of the strands of hair that will be visible.

Strands 1 and 2 (2 strands): ch29, and starting in second ch from hook: 28 sc, slst into next st of Round 5 to join.
Strands 3–9 (7 strands): ch15, and starting in second ch from hook: 14 sc, slst into next st of Round 5 to join.
Strands 10–11 (2 strands): ch29, and starting in second ch from hook: 28 sc, slst into next st of Round 5 to join.
Round 12: ch18, and starting in second ch from hook: 17 sc, slst into next st of Round 5 to join.
Strands 13–29 (17 strands): ch29, and starting in second ch from hook: 28 sc, slst into next st of Round 5 to join.
Strand 30: ch18, and starting in second ch from hook: 17 sc, slst into next st of Round 5 to join.
Fasten off and weave in ends *(19)*.

19

20

21

PART 2

Join the Black yarn into the BLO of first st of Round 3 of Part 1 *(20)*.
Strand 1: ch31, and starting in second ch from hook: 30 sc, slst BLO of next st of Round 3 to join.
Strands 2–5 (4 strands): ch17, and starting in second ch from hook: 16 sc, slst BLO of next st of Round 3 to join.
Strands 6–18 (13 strands): ch31, and starting in second ch from hook: 30 sc, slst BLO of next st of Round 3 to join.
Fasten off and weave in ends *(21)*.

PART 3

Join Black yarn to BLO of first st of Round 2 of Part 1 *(22)*.
Strands 1 and 2 (2 strands): ch18, and starting in second ch from hook: 17 sc, slst BLO of next st of Round 2 to join.
Strands 3–12 (10 strands): ch32, and starting in second ch from hook: 31 sc, slst BLO of next st of Round 2 to join.
Fasten off and weave in ends *(23)*.

ATTACH THE HAIR

Arrange the hair on the head, starting by placing the center of the MR of the hair on the center of the MR of the head. Hold in place with a pin.
Holding Parts 2 and 3 together on top of the head with hair elastic will make things easier.
Part 1: position strands 1, 2, 10, and 11 in front of the ears *(24)*.
Position strands 3–9 on the forehead *(25)*.
Position strands 12 and 30 above the ears *(26)*.
Place all the remaining strands around the head *(27)*. It does not matter if there are a few little gaps between the strands – they will be filled in later.
Stick down the strands one by one, applying glue to each strand. Hold in place with pins until the glue has dried.
Part 2: stick strands 2–5 to the forehead *(28)*.
Stick the other strands around the head *(29, 30)*.
Part 3: stick strands 1 and 2 to the forehead *(31)*.
Stick the other strands around the head *(32, 33)*.

Fox Ears (make 2)

Note: work in spiral rounds.

Using Sorbus, make MR.
Round 1: 4 sc into MR. (4 sts)
Round 2: inc 4 times. (8 sts)
Round 3: [1 sc, inc] 4 times. (12 sts)
Round 4: [2 sc, inc] 4 times. (16 sts)
Round 5: [3 sc, inc] 4 times. (20 sts)
Rounds 6–9 (4 rounds): 1 sc in each st around.
Fasten off and cut, leaving enough yarn for sewing to head.
Using Cream, embroider the inside of the ear between Rounds 4 and 9 *(34)*.
Sew one ear to each side of the head *(35, 36)*.

22

23

24

25

26

27

28

Shoes (make 2)

SOLES

Using Black, make the soles according to instructions in Standard Parts: Soles of the Shoes.

MAIN BODY OF SHOE

Join Black yarn to BLO of third slst of previous round (37).
Round 1: 25 sc BLO, slst to join. (25 sts)
Rounds 2 and 3 (2 rounds): ch1, 1 sc in each st around, slst to join.
Round 4: ch1, 7 sc [1 sc, dec] 4 times, 6 sc, slst to join. (21 sts)
Round 5: ch1, 8 sc, dec, 3 sc, dec, 6 sc, slst to join. (19 sts)
Rounds 6–8 (3 rounds): ch1, 1 sc in each st around, slst to join. (19 sts)
Round 9: ch1, 1 sc in each stitch, slst on RS to join.
Fasten off and weave in ends (38).

29 30

31

32 33 34 35

36 37 38

The Little Companions

BIG COMPANION

Body

Using Sorbus, work the body according to instructions for the big body in Standard Parts: The Little Companions.

Ears (make 2)

Note: work in spiral rounds.

Using Sorbus, make MR.
Round 1: 4 sc into MR. (4 sts)
Round 2: [1 sc, inc] twice. (6 sts)
Round 3: [2 sc, inc] twice. (8 sts)
Round 4: [3 sc, inc] 2 times. (10 sts)
Fasten off and cut, leaving enough yarn for sewing to body.
Using Cream, embroider the inside of the ear *(39)*.
Sew one ear to each side of the body between Rounds 2 and 7 *(40)*.

Tail

Note: work in spiral rounds.

Using Cream, make MR.
Round 1: 4 sc into MR. (4 sts)
Round 2: [1 sc, inc] twice. (6 sts)
Round 3: [1 sc, inc] 3 times. (9 sts)
Change to Sorbus.
Round 4: [2 sc, inc] 3 times. (12 sts)
Round 5: [1 sc, inc] 6 times. (18 sts)
Rounds 6 and 7 (2 rounds): 1 sc in each st around.
Round 8: [4 sc, dec] 3 times. (15 sts)
Round 9: [3 sc, dec] 3 times. (12 sts)
Round 10: [2 sc, dec] 3 times. (9 sts)
Stuff.
Round 11: [1 sc, dec] 3 times. (6 sts)
Flatten out the opening, then work 3 sc through both thicknesses at the same time to close.
Fasten off, leaving sufficient yarn for sewing together.
Sew the tail to the back, between Rounds 20 and 23 *(41)*.
Add some blush under the eyes *(42)*.

39 40

41

42

43

MEDIUM-SIZED COMPANION

Body

Using Sorbus, work the body according to instructions for the medium-sized body in Standard Parts: The Little Companions.

Ears (make 2)

Note: work in spiral rounds.

Using Sorbus, work as for big companion's ears.
Sew one ear to each side of the body between Rounds 2 and 7.

Tail

Note: work in spiral rounds.

Using Cream, work as for big companion's tail.
Sew the tail to the back, between Rounds 16 and 19.
Add some blush under the eyes (43).

44

SMALL COMPANION

Body

Using Sorbus, work the body according to instructions for the small body in Standard Parts: The Little Companions.

Ears (make 2)

Note: work in spiral rounds.

Using Sorbus, work as for big companion's ears.
Sew one ear to each side of the body between Rounds 1 and 6.

45

Tail

Note: work in spiral rounds.

Using Cream, work as for big companion's tail.
Sew the tail to the back, between Rounds 12 and 15.
Add some blush under the eyes (44).

Leaves (make 5)

Using Green Beryl, make MR.
Round 1: 1 sc, 1 hdc, 1 dc, 1 tr, ch3, slst into third ch from hook, 1 tr, 1 dc, 1 hdc, 1 sc into MR, slst to join.
Fasten off and weave in ends (45).

Mitsuki

Mitsuki lives in a world of lush gardens, where she loves to care for her roses. With her little companions, she whispers to the flower petals and gives them all the love they need to flourish.

Finished Size

Mitsuki: approx 8½in (21.5cm) tall
Companions: between 1¾in (4.5cm) and 2¾in (7cm) tall

Note:
Size may vary depending on your gauge (tension) and the yarn used

Tools and Materials

Yarn and Colors Must-Have yarn in the following colors:

US 4 (2.00mm) crochet hook
Fiberfill stuffing
2 x 7mm safety eyes
Basic tool kit
(see Materials)

Instructions

Note: always use X-shaped stitches and joined rounds, unless stated otherwise.

Legs (make 2)

Using Black, make MR.
Round 1: 6 sc into MR, slst to join. (6 sts)
Round 2: ch1, inc in each st around, slst to join. (12 sts)
Round 3: ch1, [1 sc, inc] 6 times, slst to join. (18 sts)
Rounds 4 and 5 (2 rounds): ch1, 1 sc in each st around, slst to join.
Round 6: ch1, 6 sc, dec 3 times, 6 sc, change to Sunglow, slst to join. (15 sts)
Round 7: ch1, 5 sc, dec, 1 sc, dec, 5 sc, slst to join. (13 sts)
Round 8: ch1, 1 sc in each st around, change to Black, slst to join.
Round 9: ch1, 1 sc in each st around, slst to join.
Round 10: ch1, 1 sc in each st around, change to Sunglow, slst to join.
Round 11: ch1, 1 sc in each st around, slst to join.
Round 12: ch1, 1 sc in each st around, change to Black, slst to join.
Round 13: ch1, 1 sc in each st around, slst to join.
Round 14: ch1, 2 sc, inc, 7 sc, inc, 2 sc, change to Sunglow, slst to join. (15 sts)
Round 15: ch1, 1 sc in each st around, slst to join.
Round 16: ch1, 1 sc in each st around, change to Black, slst to join.

Round 17: ch1, 1 sc in each st around, slst to join.
Round 18: ch1, 2 sc, dec, 7 sc, dec, 2 sc, change to Sunglow, slst to join. (13 sts)
Round 19: ch1, 2 sc, inc, 7 sc, inc, 2 sc, slst to join. (15 sts)
Stuff the foot.
Round 20: ch1, 3 sc, inc, 7 sc, inc, 3 sc, change to Black, slst to join. (17 sts)
Round 21: ch1, 1 sc in each st around, slst to join.
Round 22: ch1, 4 sc, inc, 7 sc, inc, 4 sc, change to Sunglow, slst to join. (19 sts)
Round 23: ch1, 1 sc in each st around, slst to join.
Round 24: ch1, 5 sc, inc, 7 sc, inc, 5 sc, change to Black, slst to join. (21 sts)
Round 25: ch1, 1 sc in each st around, slst to join.
Round 26: ch1, 1 sc in each st around, change to Vanilla, slst to join.
Round 27: ch1, 1 sc in each st around, slst to join.
Round 28: ch1, 1 sc in each st around, slst on RS to join.
Mark last slst.
Leg 1: fasten off and weave in ends.
Stuff leg firmly.
Leg 2: repeat steps as for leg 1, but at end, work last slst on WS. Stuff leg firmly. Do not mark last slst, do not cut yarn. Continue as follows:

Body

Note: see Diagram 2, Techniques: Joining the Legs.

Round 29: ch1, 8 sc into leg 2, ch2, [1 sc into fourth st before marked slst, 3 sc, 1 sc into same st as marked slst, 16 sc] on leg 1, 2 sc into ch2, 13 sc into remaining sts of leg 2, slst to join. (46 sts)
Round 30: ch1, 8 sc into leg 2, 2 sc in opposite side of ch2, [dec, 21 sc] on leg 1, [dec, 11 sc] on remaining sts of leg 2, slst to join. (44 sts)

Note: stuff as you go along.

Rounds 31–34 (4 rounds): ch1, 1 sc in each st around, slst to join.
Round 35: ch1, 1 sc in each st around, work an additional 10 sc in order to start next round in middle of back, slst BLO to join.
Round 36: ch1, 14 sc BLO, dec BLO, 10 sc BLO, dec BLO, 16 sc BLO, slst to join. (42 sts)
Round 37: ch1, 1 sc in each st around, slst to join.
Round 38: ch1, 13 sc, dec, 10 sc, dec, 15 sc, change to Sunglow. (40 sts)
Round 39: slst BLO of each st around.
Round 40: 1 sc BLO of each st around, slst to join.
Round 41: ch1, [8 sc, dec] 4 times, slst to join. (36 sts)
Rounds 42 and 43 (2 rounds): ch1, 1 sc in each st around, slst to join.
Round 44: ch1, [7 sc, dec] 4 times, slst to join. (32 sts)
Round 45: ch1, 1 sc in each st around, slst to join.
Round 46: ch1, [6 sc, dec] 4 times, slst to join. (28 sts)
Round 47: ch1, 1 sc in each st around, slst to join.
Round 48: ch1, [5 sc, dec] 4 times, slst to join. (24 sts)
Round 49: ch1, 1 sc in each st around, change to Ecru, slst BLO to join.
Round 50: ch1, 6 sc BLO, dec BLO, 10 sc BLO, dec BLO, 4 sc BLO, slst to join. (22 sts)
Round 51: ch1, 1 sc in each st around, slst to join.
Round 52: ch1, 6 sc, dec, 10 sc, dec, 2 sc, slst to join. (20 sts)
Round 53: ch1, [3 sc, dec] 4 times, slst to join. (16 sts)
Round 54: ch1, [3 sc, dec] twice, 4 sc, dec, slst to join. (13 sts)
Rounds 55–65 (11 rounds): ch1, 1 sc in each st around, slst to join.
Round 66: ch1, 5 sc, dec, 6 sc, slst to join. (12 sts)

Note: strengthen the neck (see Techniques: Strengthening the Neck).

Round 67: ch1, dec 6 times, slst to join. (6 sts)
Cut the yarn and fasten off (1).

COLLAR

Holding the body neck down, join Vanilla yarn to FLO of first st of Round 49 (2).

Round 1: [ch2, slst FLO of each st] 24 times.

Fasten off and weave in ends (3).

HEART

Note: work in spiral rounds.

Using Vanilla, make MR.

Round 1: ch3, 2 dc, 1 hdc, 1 sc, ch2, 1 sc, 1 hdc, 2 dc, ch3, slst into MR.

Round 2: 2 slst into ch3-sp, 9 slst, 2 slst into ch3-sp.

Fasten off and cut, leaving enough yarn for sewing to body.

Sew the heart to center front of body (4).

Skirt

PART 1 (MAKE 14)

Note: work Part 1 around a foundation chain.

Using Marble, ch11 and start in third ch from hook.

Round 1: 8 dc, 4 dc into last ch to pass to other side of foundation chain, 8 dc, slst on RS to join. (20 sts)

Fasten off, leaving sufficient yarn for sewing to body (5).

Sew each part under the FLOs of sts in Round 35 (6, 7).

PART 2

Note: work Part 2 along a foundation chain.

Using Vanilla, ch53 and start in second ch from hook.

Row 1: 2 slst, [ch3, slst into third ch from hook, 4 slst] 12 times, ch3, slst into third ch from hook, 2 slst.

Fasten off, leaving sufficient yarn for sewing to body (8).

Sew on just above the petals (9).

1

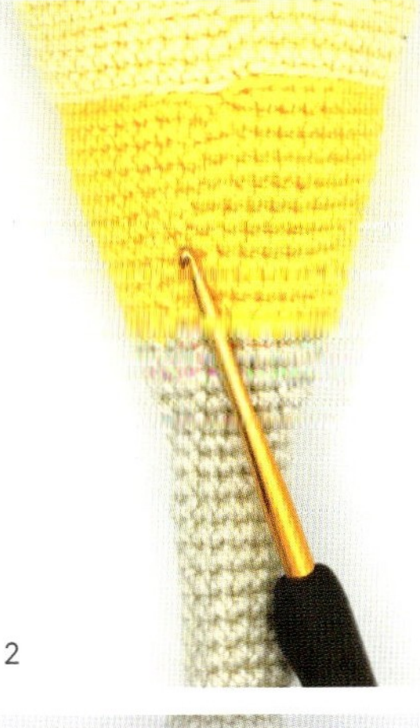
2

3

4

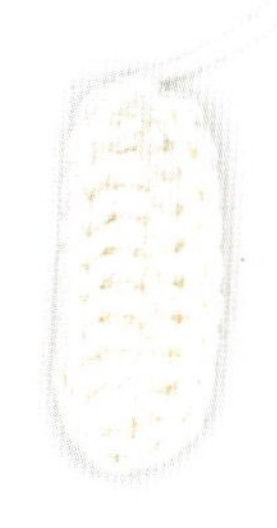
5

6

7

8

9

Arms (make 2)

Using Ecru, make MR.
Round 1: 6 sc into MR, slst to join. (6 sts)
Round 2: ch1, [1 sc, inc] 3 times, slst to join. (9 sts)
Round 3: ch1, [2 sc, inc] 3 times, slst to join. (12 sts)
Round 4: ch1, 1 sc in each st around, slst to join.
Round 5: ch1, 5 sc, dec, 5 sc, slst to join. (11 sts)
Round 6: ch1, 5 sc, 1 3sc-bo (= thumb), 5 sc, slst to join.
Round 7: ch1, 5 sc, dec, 2 sc, dec, slst to join. (9 sts)
Round 8: ch1, 1 sc in each st around, slst to join.
Round 9: ch1, 5 sc, dec, 2 sc, slst to join. (8 sts)
Stuff hand firmly.
Rounds 10–18 (9 rounds): ch1, 1 sc in each st around, slst to join.
Round 19: ch1, 4 sc, dec, 2 sc, slst to join. (7 sts)
Rounds 20–24 (5 rounds): ch1, 1 sc in each st around, slst to join.
Stuff the arms lightly halfway.
Flatten out the opening, then work 3 sc through both thicknesses at the same time to close.
Fasten off and cut, leaving enough yarn for sewing to body.
Sew one arm to each side of the body between Rounds 52 and 53, ensuring that the thumbs are positioned at the front *(10, 11)*.

10

11

12

13

Wings (make 2)

Note: work the wings in ovals around a foundation chain.

Using Marble, ch15 and start in second ch from hook.
Round 1: 13 sc, (4 sc) into last ch to pass to other side of foundation chain, 12 sc, inc. (31 sts)
Round 2: inc twice, 11 sc, inc 4 times, 12 sc, inc twice. (39 sts)
Round 3: [1 sc, inc] twice, 4 sc, 4 hdc, 3 dc, [dc-inc, 1 dc] 4 times, 3 dc, 4 hdc, 4 sc, [inc, 1 sc] twice, inc. (48 sts)
Cut the yarn and work an invisible finish *(12)*.
Using Marble, ch15 and start in second ch from hook.
Repeat Rounds 1–3 but do not cut the yarn.
Continue working into both pieces, WS together.
Round 4: 48 slst. (48 sts)
Fasten off and cut, leaving enough yarn for sewing to body.
Sew the wings to the back *(14)*.

14

Head

Using Ecru, make MR.
Round 1: 6 sc into MR, slst to join. (6 sts)
Round 2: ch1, inc in each st around, slst to join. (12 sts)
Round 3: ch1, [1 sc, inc] 6 times, slst to join. (18 sts)
Round 4: ch1, [1 sc, inc, 1 sc] 6 times, slst to join. (24 sts)
Round 5: ch1, [3 sc, inc] 6 times, slst to join. (30 sts)
Round 6: ch1, [2 sc, inc, 2 sc] 6 times, slst to join. (36 sts)
Round 7: ch1, [5 sc, inc] 6 times, slst to join. (42 sts)

Round 8: ch1, [3 sc, inc, 3 sc] 6 times, slst to join. (48 sts)
Round 9: ch1, [7 sc, inc] 6 times, slst to join. (54 sts)
Round 10: ch1, [4 sc, inc, 4 sc] 6 times, slst to join. (60 sts)
Round 11: ch1, 1 sc in each st around, slst to join.
Round 12: ch1, [9 sc, inc] 6 times, slst to join. (66 sts)
Round 13: ch1, 1 sc in each st around, slst to join.
Round 14: ch1, 16 sc, inc, 32 sc, inc, 16 sc, slst to join. (68 sts)
Rounds 15–23 (9 rounds): ch1, 1 sc in each st around, slst to join.
Round 24: ch1, 28 sc, ch1, sk 1 st, 10 sc, ch1, sk 1 st, 28 sc, slst to join.
Round 25: ch1, 28 sc, 1 sc into ch, 10 sc, 1 sc into ch, 28 sc, slst to join.
Round 26: ch1, 16 sc, dec, 32 sc, dec, 16 sc, slst to join. (66 sts)
Round 27: ch1, 1 sc in each st around, slst to join.
Round 28: ch1, 15 sc, dec, 32 sc, dec, 15 sc, slst to join. (64 sts)
Insert the eyes into the holes formed by the skipped sts in Round 24.
Round 29: ch1, [14 sc, dec] 4 times, slst to join. (60 sts)
Round 30: ch1, [4 sc, dec, 4 sc] 6 times, slst to join. (54 sts)
Round 31: ch1, [7 sc, dec] 6 times, slst to join. (48 sts)
Round 32: ch1, [4 sc, dec] 8 times, slst to join. (40 sts)
Round 33: ch1, [3 sc, dec] 8 times, slst to join. (32 sts)
Start to stuff.
Round 34: ch1, [2 sc, dec] 8 times, slst to join. (24 sts)
Round 35: ch1, [1 sc, dec] 8 times, slst BLO to join. (16 sts)
Round 36: ch1, 1 sc BLO of each st around, slst to join.
Rounds 37–41 (5 rounds): ch1, 1 sc in each st around, slst to join.
Fasten off and weave in ends. Complete the stuffing.
Push Rounds 36–41 inside the head (15).
Using White floss, embroider the whites of the eyes (16), then add a touch of Blue floss to the sides of the eyes (17).
Using Black floss, embroider the black above the eyes and finish by embroidering the eyelashes (18).
Using Brown floss, embroider the eyebrows between Rounds 20 and 22 (19).
Using Ecru, embroider the nose between Rounds 26 and 27. Use a brush and some blush to add a little color to the cheeks and above the nose (20).

Note: the circumference of the head once stuffed is approximately 7½in (19cm).

EARS (MAKE 2)

Using Ecru, make MR.
Round 1: 1 sc, 4 hdc, 1 sc into MR. (6 sts)
Fasten off, leaving sufficient yarn for sewing to head.
Sew one ear to each side of the head between Rounds 23 and 27, leaving a gap of 8 sts between ear and eye (21, 22).

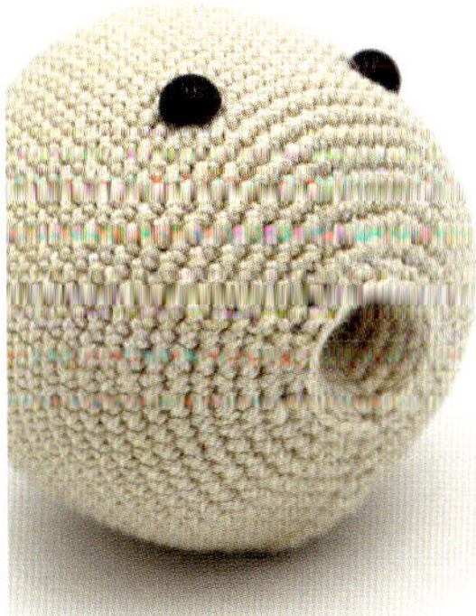
15

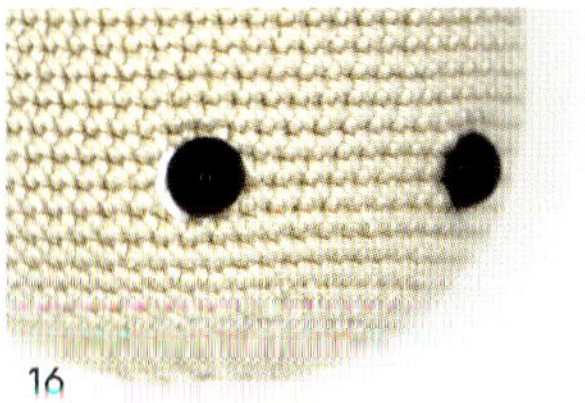
16

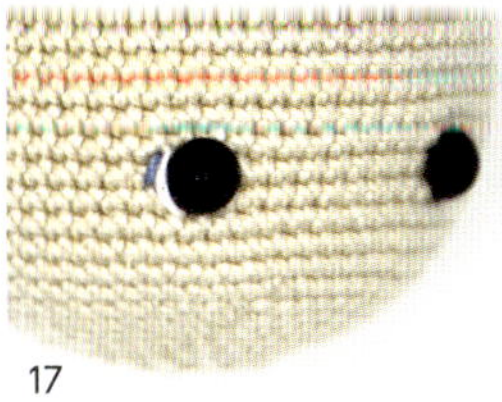
17

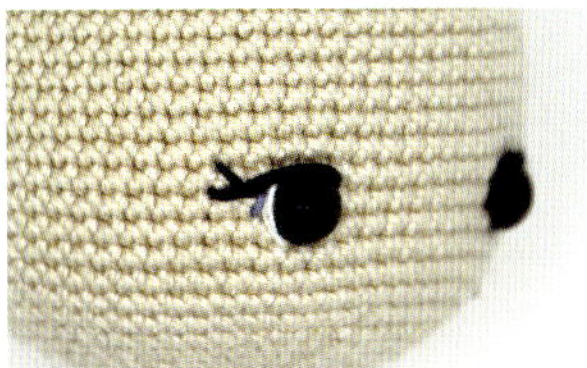
18

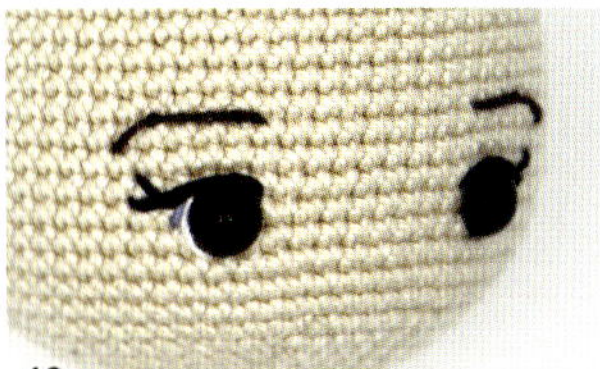
19

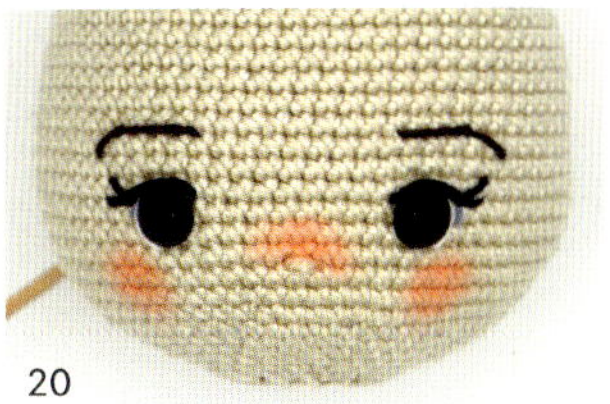
20

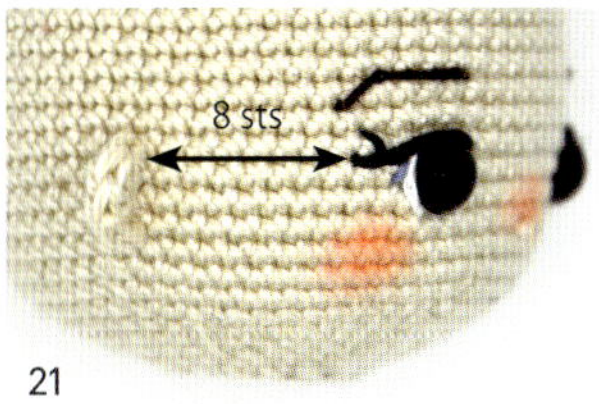

21

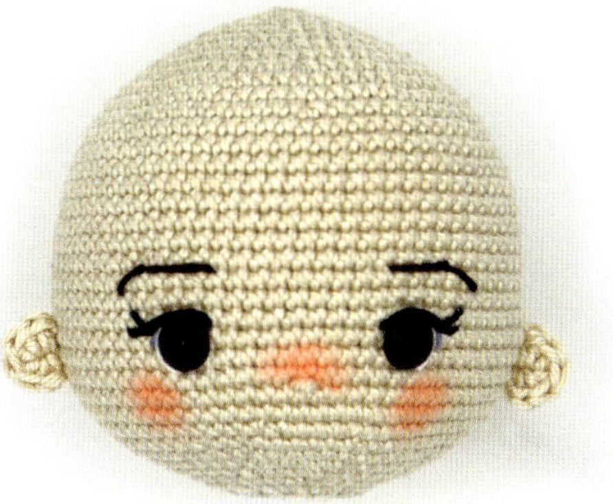
22

ATTACH THE HEAD

Using Ecru, attach the head according to instructions in Techniques: Attaching the Head. Leave 7 rounds in Ecru visible.

Hair

PART 1

Using Bronze, make MR.
Round 1: 6 sc into MR, slst to join. (6 sts)
Round 2: ch1, inc in each st around, slst FLO to join. (12 sts)
Round 3: ch1, [1 sc FLO, inc FLO] 6 times, slst FLO to join. (18 sts)
Round 4: ch1, [1 sc FLO, inc FLO, 1 sc FLO] 6 times, slst to join. (24 sts)
Round 5: ch1, [3 sc, inc] 6 times, slst to join. (30 sts)
Do not cut the yarn. Continue with the strands of hair.

Note: it is the WS of the strands of hair that will be visible.

Strands 1 and 2 (2 strands): ch35, and starting in second ch from hook: slst, 33 sc, slst into next st of Round 5 to join.
Strand 3: ch19, and starting in second ch from hook: slst, 17 sc, slst into next st of Round 5 to join.
Strands 4–9 (6 strands): ch16, and starting in second ch from hook: slst, 14 sc, slst into next st of Round 5 to join.
Strand 10: repeat strand 3.
Strands 11 and 12 (2 strands): repeat strands 1 and 2.
Strand 13: ch35, and starting in second ch from hook: slst, 33 sc, slst into next st of Round 5 to join.
Strand 14: ch35, and starting in second ch from hook: slst, 33 sc, slst into same st where last slst of previous strand was worked (you now have 2 strands in the same st).
Strand 15: ch35, and starting in second ch from hook: slst, 33 sc, slst into next st of Round 5 to join.
Strands 16–18 (3 strands): repeat strands 13–15.
Strands 19–21 (3 strands): repeat strands 13–15.
Strands 22–24 (3 strands): repeat strands 13–15.
Strands 25–27 (3 strands): repeat strands 13–15.
Strands 28–30 (3 strands): repeat strands 13–15.
Strands 31–33 (3 strands): repeat strands 13–15.
Strands 34–36 (3 strands): repeat strands 13–15.
Strands 37–39 (3 strands): repeat strands 13–15.
Fasten off and weave in ends *(23)*.

PART 2

Join Bronze yarn to BLO of first st of Round 3 of Part 1 *(24)*.
Strand 1: ch39, and starting in second ch from hook: slst, 37 sc, slst BLO of next st of Round 3 to join.
Strands 2–5 (4 strands): ch23, and starting in second ch from hook: slst, 21 sc, slst BLO of next st of Round 3 to join.
Strands 6–18 (13 strands): repeat strand 1.
Fasten off and weave in ends *(25)*.

23

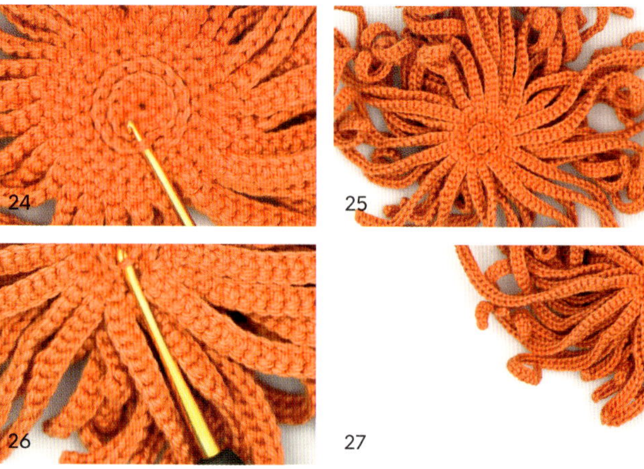

24 25 26 27

28

29

30

31

PART 3

Join Bronze yarn to BLO of first st of Round 2 of Part 1 (26).
Strands 1 and 2 (2 strands): ch25, and starting in second ch from hook: slst, 23 sc, slst BLO of next st of Round 2 to join.
Strands 3–12 (10 strands): ch41, and starting in second ch from hook: slst, 39 sc, slst BLO of next st of Round 2 to join.
Fasten off and weave in ends (27).

ATTACH THE HAIR

Arrange the hair on the head, starting by placing the center of the MR of the hair on the center of the MR of the head. Hold in place with a pin.
Holding Parts 2 and 3 together on top of the head with hair elastic will make things easier.
Part 1: position strands 1, 2, 11, and 12 in front of the ears (28).
Stick down the strands one by one, applying glue to each strand. Hold in place with pins until the glue has dried.
Glue strands 3–10 to the forehead (29).
Glue all the remaining strands around the head (30). It does not matter if there are a few little gaps between the strands– they will be filled in later.
Twist the very end of each strand (31).
Part 2: twist and glue strands 2–5 to the forehead (32).
Glue the remaining strands around the head (33).
Twist the very end of each strand (34).
Part 3: twist and stick strands 1 and 2 to the forehead (35).
Glue the remaining strands around the head (36).
Twist the very end of each strand (37).

Headband

Note: work the headband along a foundation chain.

Using Black, ch37 and start in second ch from hook.
Row 1: ch1, 1 sc, 32 hdc, 1 sc, slst to join. (36 sts)
Fasten off, leaving sufficient yarn for sewing to head.
Sew the headband to the head (38, 39).

32 33

34

35

36 37

38

39

BEE ANTENNAE (MAKE 2)

Note: work the antennae along a foundation chain.

Using Black, ch10 and starting in third ch from hook.
Row 1: (1 dc, slst) into same st, 7 slst.
Fasten off, leaving sufficient yarn for sewing to headband.
Sew the antennae to the headband, stiffening with glue if desired *(40)*.

Shoes (make 2)

SOLES

Using Black, make the soles according to instructions in Standard Parts: Soles of the Shoes.

MAIN BODY OF SHOE

Join Black yarn to BLO of third slst of previous round *(41)*.
Round 1: 1 sc BLO of each st around, slst to join. (25 sts)
Rounds 2 and 3 (2 rounds): ch1, 1 sc in each st around, slst to join.
Round 4: ch1, 7 sc, [1 hdc, 1 hdc dec] 4 times, 1 hdc, 5 sc, change to Marble. (21 sts)
Round 5: slst in each st around.
Round 6: [slst BLO, ch2] 21 times.
Fasten off and weave in ends *(42)*.

Flowers

FLOWER (MAKE 3)

Note: work the flower along a foundation chain.

Make 1 flower each using Cotton Candy, Peony Pink, and Vanilla.

Ch22 and start in second ch from hook.
Row 1: [2 sc, (1 hdc, ch2, slst into second ch from hook, 1 hdc into same st)] 7 times.
Roll the chain up to form 1 flower and sew through all the layers together.
Fasten off and weave in ends *(43)*.

STALK

Cut a 1½in (4cm) length of aluminum wire, diameter 0.2in (0.5cm).
Wrap Grass yarn around it, leaving the 2 ends free *(44)* and hold in place with strong glue.
Stick the flower to the stem *(45)*.

LEAF

Note: work the leaf along a foundation chain.

Using Grass, ch3 and start in second ch from hook.
Row 1: slst, 1 sc.
Fasten off and weave in ends.
Stick the flower to the stem *(46)*.

40

41

42

43

44

45

46

47

The Little Companions

BIG COMPANION

Body

Using Sunglow, make MR.
Round 1: 6 sc into MR, slst to join. (6 sts)
Round 2: ch1, inc 6 times, slst to join. (12 sts)
Round 3: ch1, [1 sc, inc] 6 times, slst to join. (18 sts)
Round 4: ch1, [1 sc, inc, 1 sc] 6 times, slst to join. (24 sts)
Round 5: ch1, 1 sc in each st around, slst to join.
Round 6: ch1, [7 sc, inc] 3 times, slst to join. (27 sts)
Round 7: ch1, 1 sc in each st around, slst to join.
Round 8: ch1, [4 sc, inc, 4 sc] 3 times, slst to join. (30 sts)
Round 9: ch1, 1 sc in each st around, slst to join.
Round 10: ch1, [9 sc, inc] 3 times, slst to join. (33 sts)
Round 11: ch1, 1 sc in each st around, slst to join.
Round 12: ch1, [5 sc, inc, 5 sc] 3 times, slst to join. (36 sts)
Round 13: ch1, 1 sc in each st around, change to Black, slst to join.
Round 14: ch1, [11 sc, inc] 3 times, slst to join. (39 sts)
Round 15: ch1, 1 sc in each st around, change to Sunglow, slst to join.
Round 16: ch1, [6 sc, inc, 6 sc] 3 times, slst to join. (42 sts)
Round 17: ch1, 1 sc in each st around, change to Black, slst to join.
Round 18: ch1, [13 sc, inc] 3 times, slst to join. (45 sts)
Round 19: ch1, 1 sc in each st around, change to Sunglow, slst to join.
Round 20: ch1, [7 sc, inc, 7 sc] 3 times, slst to join. (48 sts)
Round 21: ch1, 1 sc in each st around, change to Black, slst to join. (48 sts)
Round 22: ch1, 1 sc in each st around, slst to join.
Round 23: ch1, [6 sc, dec] 6 times, change to Sunglow, slst to join. (42 sts)
Round 24: ch1, [5 sc, dec] 6 times, slst BLO to join. (36 sts)
Round 25: ch1, [4 sc BLO, dec BLO] 6 times, slst to join. (30 sts)
Round 26: ch1, [3 sc, dec] 6 times, slst to join. (24 sts)
Round 27: ch1, [2 sc, dec] 6 times, slst to join. (18 sts)
Stuff.
Round 28: ch1, [1 sc, dec] 6 times, slst to join. (12 sts)
Round 29: ch1, dec 6 times, slst to join. (6 sts)
Cut the yarn and fasten off.
Using Black floss, embroider the eyes on Round 10, leaving a gap of 4 sts between them.
Using White floss, embroider 1 stitch in each eye.

48

49

Antennae (make 2)

Note: work the antennae along a foundation chain.

Using Black, ch6.
Row 1: (1 sc, slst) into second ch from hook, 4 slst.
Fasten off and cut, leaving enough yarn for sewing to body.
Sew the antennae on top of the body at Round 2 (47).

Wings (make 2)

Note: work the wings in ovals around a foundation chain.

Using Marble, ch13 and start in third ch from hook.
Round 1: 10 dc, (4 dc) into last ch to pass to other side of foundation chain, 10 dc, slst on RS to join. (24 sts)
Fasten off, leaving sufficient yarn for sewing to body.
Sew the wings to the back, between Rounds 15 and 19 (48).
Add some blush under the eyes (49).

MEDIUM-SIZED COMPANION

Body

Using Sunglow, make MR.
Round 1: 6 sc into MR, slst to join. (6 sts)
Round 2: ch1, inc 6 times, slst to join. (12 sts)
Round 3: ch1, [1 sc, inc] 6 times, slst to join. (18 sts)
Round 4: ch1, [1 sc, inc, 1 sc] 6 times, slst to join. (24 sts)
Round 5: ch1, 1 sc in each st around, slst to join.
Round 6: ch1, [7 sc, inc] 3 times, slst to join. (27 sts)
Round 7: ch1, 1 sc in each st around, slst to join.
Round 8: ch1, [4 sc, inc, 4 sc] 3 times, slst to join. (30 sts)
Round 9: ch1, 1 sc in each st around, slst to join.
Round 10: ch1, [9 sc, inc] 3 times, slst to join. (33 sts)
Round 11: ch1, 1 sc in each st around, change to Black, slst to join.
Round 12: ch1, [5 sc, inc, 5 sc] 3 times, slst to join. (36 sts)
Round 13: ch1, 1 sc in each st around, change to Sunglow, slst to join.
Round 14: ch1, [11 sc, inc] 3 times, slst to join. (39 sts)
Round 15: ch1, 1 sc in each st around, change to Black, slst to join.
Round 16: ch1, [6 sc, inc, 6 sc] 3 times, slst to join. (42 sts)
Round 17: ch1, 1 sc in each st around, change to Sunglow, slst to join.
Round 18: ch1, 1 sc in each st around, slst to join.
Round 19: ch1, [5 sc, dec] 6 times, change to Black, slst to join. (36 sts)
Round 20: ch1, (4 sc, dec) 6 times, change to Sunglow, slst BLO to join. (30 sts)
Round 21: ch1, [3 sc BLO, dec BLO] 6 times, slst to join. (24 sts)
Round 22: ch1, [2 sc, dec] 6 times, slst to join. (18 sts)
Stuff.
Round 23: ch1, [1 sc, dec] 6 times, slst to join. (12 sts)
Round 24: ch1, dec 6 times, slst to join. (6 sts)
Cut the yarn and fasten off.
Using Black floss, embroider the eyes on Round 8, leaving a gap of 4 sts between them.
Using White floss, embroider 1 stitch in each eye.

Antennae (make 2)

Note: work the antennae along a foundation chain.

Using Black, ch5 and start in second ch from hook.
Row 1: (1 sc, slst) into second ch from hook, 3 slst.
Fasten off and cut, leaving enough yarn for sewing to body.
Sew the antennae to the top of the body at Round 2.

Wings (make 2)

Note: work the wings in ovals around a foundation chain.

Using Marble, ch11 and start in third ch from hook.
Round 1: 8 dc, (4 dc) into last ch to pass to other side of foundation chain, 8 dc, slst on RS to join. (20 sts)
Fasten off, leaving sufficient yarn for sewing to body.
Sew the wings to the back, between Rounds 12 and 16.
Add some blush under the eyes (50).

SMALL COMPANION

Body

Using Sunglow, make MR.
Round 1: 6 sc into MR, slst to join. (6 sts)
Round 2: ch1, inc 6 times, slst to join. (12 sts)
Round 3: ch1, [1 sc, inc] 6 times, slst to join. (18 sts)
Round 4: ch1, [1 sc, inc, 1 sc] 6 times, slst to join.
Round 5: ch1, 1 sc in each st around, slst to join. (24 sts)
Round 6: ch1, [7 sc, inc] 3 times, slst to join. (27 sts)
Round 7: ch1, 1 sc in each st around, slst to join.
Round 8: ch1, [4 sc, inc, 4 sc] 3 times, slst to join. (30 sts)
Round 9: ch1, 1 sc in each st around, slst to join. (30 sts)
Round 10: ch1, [9 sc, inc] 3 times, slst to join. (33 sts)
Round 11: ch1, 1 sc in each st around, change to Black, slst to join.
Round 12: ch1, [5 sc, inc, 5 sc] 3 times, slst to join. (36 sts)
Round 13: ch1, 1 sc in each st around, change to Sunglow, slst to join.
Round 14: ch1, 1 sc in each st around, slst to join.
Round 15: ch1, (4 sc, dec) 6 times, change to Black, slst to join. (30 sts)
Round 16: ch1, [3 sc, dec] 6 times, change to Sunglow, slst BLO to join. (24 sts)
Round 17: ch1, [2 sc BLO, dec BLO] 6 times, slst to join. (18 sts)
Stuff.
Round 18: ch1, [1 sc, dec] 6 times, slst to join. (12 sts)
Round 19: ch1, dec 6 times, slst to join. (6 sts)
Cut the yarn and fasten off.
Using Black floss, embroider the eyes on Round 8, leaving a gap of 4 sts between them.
Using White floss, embroider 1 stitch in each eye.

Antennae (make 2)

Note: work the antennae along a foundation chain.

Using Black, ch4.
Row 1: (1 sc, slst) into second ch from hook, 2 slst.
Fasten off and cut, leaving enough yarn for sewing to body.
Sew the antennae to the top of the body at Round 2.

Wings (make 2)

Note: work the wings in ovals around a foundation chain.

Using Marble, ch9 and start in third ch from hook.
Round 1: 6 dc, (4 dc) into last ch to pass to other side of foundation chain, 6 dc, slst on RS to join. (16 sts)
Fasten off, leaving sufficient yarn for sewing to body.
Sew the wings to the back between Rounds 9 and 13.
Add some blush under the eyes (51).

50

51

Thanks

First of all, a big thank you to my children who inspire me every day. I am so grateful for their unfailing support, their advice, and their encouraging hugs. Thanks to Noah for his kindness and interminable conversations. Thanks to Éléonore for all her kisses and her precious help in choosing the colors (you might not believe it, but I have a touch of color blindness).

Thank you to my husband – without him I would never have started on the *Kawaii Crochet Dolls* adventure. Without him, I could never have turned my passion into my job.

Thank you to my nearest and dearest, my mom, my dad, my three little sisters, my aunt Maryse, my uncle Gérald, and my friend Cécile who has always believed in me and whom I know will always be there to encourage and support me.

Thanks to Viviane, my editor, for giving me this awesome opportunity to write my first book. Thanks to Marine for her kindness and support throughout the writing of this book.

Thank you to Yarn and Colors, our partner on this project, for all their balls of yarn in such beautiful colors, which I love transforming into beautiful dolls.

And thank you to my dear crocheting friends, Justine [@la.fabrique.a.ju] and Emelyne [@les_rouspetteries_demmy], for all their excellent advice, their sharp eyes, and their good humor. Thank you to Justine for having been my right hand throughout these long months of creation. We had such fun!

And finally, thanks to all of you who follow me on social media and have given me your encouragement every day. I can't wait to see this book come to life on your crochet hooks!

Elise

A DAVID AND CHARLES BOOK

David and Charles is an imprint of David and Charles, Ltd
Suite A, Tourism House, Pynes Hill, Exeter, EX2 5WS

EU GPSR Authorised Representative:
Logos Europe, 9 rue Nicolas Poussin, 17000, La Rochelle, France
Email: Contact@logoseurope.eu

First published in France as *Les Poupées de P'tite Peste au Crochet* in 2025
This edition first published in the UK and USA in 2026

A catalogue record for this book is available from the British Library.

ISBN-13: 9781446317693 paperback
ISBN-13: 9781446317709 EPUB

This book has been printed on paper from approved suppliers and made from pulp from sustainable sources

Printed in China through Asia Pacific Offset for:
David and Charles, Ltd
Suite A, Tourism House, Pynes Hill, Exeter, EX2 5WS

10 9 8 7 6 5 4 3 2 1

Publishing Director: Ame Verso
Publishing Manager: Jeni Chown
Project Editor: Rachael Prest
Editorial Assistant: Jenna McGill
Translation: Tankerton Translations
Text, Designs and Photography: Elise Brocard
Page Layout: Christine Lim
Pre-press Designer: Susan Reansbury
Illustrations: Céline Cantat
Production Manager: Beverley Richardson

David and Charles publishes high-quality books on a wide range of subjects. For more information visit www.davidandcharles.com.

Share your makes with us on social media using #dandcbooks and follow us on Facebook and Instagram by searching for @dandcbooks.

Layout of the digital edition of this book may vary depending on reader hardware and display settings.